how to start a home-based

Etsy Business

Gina Luker

Foreword by
Myquillyn Smith (TheNester.com)

gpp®

Guilford, Connecticut

Editorial Director: Cynthia Hughes Cullen
Editor: Meredith Dias
Project Editor: Lauren Brancato
Text Design: Sheryl P. Kober
Layout Artist: Sue Murray

ISBN 978-0-7627-8483-7

Printed in the United States of America

10 9 8 7 6 5 4 3 2 1

To my husband, Mitch—the defender of my dreams

Contents

Acknowledgments

Writing a book has been a dream of mine since I was a little girl, and I'm so honored to have this opportunity. There are so many people who have helped me along the way, including my wonderful husband; our children, Lauren, Hannah, Jamie, and Tyler; my grandson, Brady; my parents; and my sister, Heather.

Besides my family, I have an entire network of friends, all of whom provided inspiration and growth for me and my story: Angie Holden, Andrea Cammarata, Lisa Pennington, Polly Blair, Karen Watson, Jennifer Rizzo, Myquillyn Smith, Kate Riley, Lindsay Ballard, Roeshel Summerville, Georgia Mallory, Mariah Clifton, Krystal Green, Ashley Mills, and all my DIYing Divas.

I would also like to thank my amazing editors, Meredith Dias and Tracee Williams, along with all of the staff at Globe Pequot Press.

Last, I'd like to thank my blog readers, customers, followers, fans, and friends who have encouraged me and cheered me along on all of my journeys. Without you, I may never have had this opportunity. I appreciate all of the years of support, friendship, and handmade love.

Foreword

For every dreamer in the world, there's a realist right around the corner armed with facts and warnings and logic and percentages. For every optimist there's a pessimist. For every person who has taken a risk, there is someone who has never tried because the idea of failure was so debilitating that he or she decided that the risk wasn't worth failing for.

Whether you are a dreamer or a realist, optimist or pessimist, risk taker or risk avoider, disappointed Etsy shop owner or just starting out and full of questions, you deserve to know what it takes to start a successful Etsy business. You've made it far enough to do the research, so you are off to a great start!

When I first opened an Etsy shop in 2008, I knew as close to nothing about running an online business as a person possibly could. All I cared about was creating pretty things and stumbling upon people who liked them enough to part with their cash. I never even thought about how I would ship my items until the day after my first sale. I was blissfully naive. If I had known that there was a secret world of intricacies and tips to running an Etsy shop, I probably would have been so overwhelmed I would have quit before I started—there were no guides, no books, no one to coach me.

You picked up this book because you are smarter than I was.

Congratulations, you are a dreamer with a creative mind who is wise enough to recognize that there's more to running a successful online shop than having the next cute idea or an overflow of stuff that someone might want. The online world is changing, and to get noticed in a way that results in sales, you know you need a plan and a mentor, someone who's been there, done that, learned the hard way, and succeeded. Someone like Gina.

Gina and I connected online first, then on the phone, where I was surprised at how eager she was to help me with product pricing. We've met up a few times in person through the years, and I've often wished I had her natural ability to think both "businessly" and creatively. She understands both worlds. It's a rare gift.

I remember watching Gina's Etsy shop in wonder as items sold daily. Gina didn't invent some new gadget that everyone wanted; she simply sold her beautifully made items really well. I wondered what her secret was. After reading this book, I know. It's not an impossible task; it's simply rare that Etsy shop owners both know what to do and care enough to actually follow through. That's the secret I wish I knew six years ago.

Instead of spending your limited time learning the hard way, you can crack open this book full of hard-earned wisdom and learn the tips and tricks to starting and growing your Etsy shop. There's room for everyone on Etsy; the question is, will you do what it takes to get noticed, and do you know how to properly conduct your business so that you can enjoy the spoils of running a successful online shop? Turn the page to get started now.

—Myquillyn Smith, TheNester.com

August 2013

Introduction

In April 2009, my husband and I had been remodeling my childhood home for several weeks, and I decided to start a blog to catalog all of the changes and progress. I thought of it as a virtual scrapbook, one that would be there for years to come so my children could look back to see where they came from. Blogging alone isn't much fun, so I tiptoed into the land of other bloggers, reaching out and leaving comments on blogs similar to mine.

We were the weird couple in our small group of friends, the people who would rather rip up floors or paint walls than go to dinner on a Saturday night. When I ventured out and found other bloggers, I found like-minded people who shared the same passions I do. Very quickly, my small blog began to find a following with readers who loved all the DIY projects I shared on a regular basis.

About three months after I started blogging, my readers began asking, "Are you ever going to open an Etsy shop?" I knew very little about the website but was intrigued by the idea of selling handmade goods, so I did some research and realized that it would be a great place to set up shop. Within a few weeks, I had my shop open for business and was creating items similar to those found in my own home, which were made primarily from the scraps left over from our remodeling efforts.

Because we had put the bulk of our money into remodeling, I had very little to put into opening up a shop. As my items began to sell, though, I grew my little shop. A few short months later, only one year after starting my blog, my side business built from nothing was generating a larger income than my full-time job working at a newspaper. Twelve short months after starting a business without even realizing it, I turned in my notice to quit my day job.

And it's been a whirlwind ever since.

In the years that have followed, I've been blessed to sell to customers all over the map, see my items be sold in stores around the globe, and even be featured in a few magazines, both national and international.

But my story isn't about pipe dreams or bragging about how far I've come. My hope is that you will see this as the journey of an average girl with average skills, who built up a business to above-average success. Within this book I will share the knowledge, experience, and even some of the trials that helped me to grow a handmade business, all through the wonderful world of Etsy.

While my path to success on selling through Etsy heavily involved blogging, this isn't the only way to find your own customer base and grow your business. My blog was a jumping-off point to grow, even if I didn't realize it from the start. There were a lot of great accidents, things I chose to do because they felt organically right to me—and happened to be exactly what I needed.

No matter where you live, what your circumstances, or how much you have to invest, there is room for you to grow a business on Etsy. With a plethora of customers who value handmade goods, need craft supplies, and covet vintage items, if your business can fit into the parameters of Etsy, you can carve out a place to build your own success story.

Meet the Stellar Sellers and Experts

Andrea Camaratta has been selling handmade goods online for nearly twenty years, many of them on Etsy. She began selling on Etsy in 2008 and has had many different successful shops along the way, including her current shop, The Cottage Market. She has been featured in numerous publications all over the world. You can find her personal blog at thecottagemarket.com.

Courtney Jeffries started her personalized pillow boutique in July 2012 to create a little corner of the Internet where shoppers could find a gift with a personalized touch. As a navy wife and mom, she wanted a career with flexible hours that could move whenever she needed. She and her husband have one child, one dog, and lots of addresses and love.

Lisa Pennington has always sought to make her surroundings beautiful. Opening an Etsy shop, Shop 24, in 2010 was the perfect extension of what she was already doing with her life: creating a lovely home and teaching her nine children. Together, she and her daughters have built a thriving business selling both online and in local shops. Her dream is to pass the shop on to her daughters when they leave home. You can read more about her family on her blog, thepenningtonpoint.com.

Jennifer Rizzo is the owner and artist of Jennifer Rizzo Design Company. She loves the excitement of making and designing handmade, one-of-a-kind home decor and sells on her Etsy shop under her own name. She has been selling her products and wholesaling to retail shops and boutiques since 2006 and began selling on Etsy in 2009. She has been featured in publications such as *Country Living* magazine, *Romantic Homes, This Old House,* and *Somerset Home.* You can find her at her lifestyle blog, jenniferrizzo.com.

James Pennington is a certified public accountant and a homeschooling father of nine. He and his wife, Lisa, have been married since 1986 and live on a small family farm in the Texas Hill Country. He has been serving churches, nonprofit organizations, individuals, and businesses since 1988 in the areas of bookkeeping, accounting, tax preparation, and representation of taxpayers before the IRS Examination and Appeals Divisions.

01 What Is Etsy?

Imagine stumbling upon the absolute best craft fair, vintage show, and supplies store you've ever encountered in your life. What if you could go there any time, day or night, from anywhere in the world, and do it in your pajamas? That is the magical world of Etsy. Shopping on Etsy is quite delightful; you can find whatever in the world makes your heart sing—no matter if it's bad 1970s fashion, upscale home decor, or one-of-a-kind, high-end art. Shopping on Etsy is wonderful, but selling is even better; the mega-website is a huge market whose audience is ready to buy.

Besides being a marketplace for buyers and sellers, Etsy is a community filled with artisans from all walks of life—from potters to bakers to jewelry makers—who connect to one another for support, ideas, and inspiration. The resources throughout the site come from not only the shop owners, but also Etsy headquarters. The website, with its young, fresh vibe, attracts more than just random *stuff*; it has become a beacon of lifestyle experts who are on the pulse of their mainstream audience.

Etsy found its audience the old-fashioned way: through word of mouth. Originator Robert Kalin knew when he started the website in June 2005 that if he built a brand by putting the focus on the customer, then those customers would in turn promote it. Kalin explains, "When you have a service that people feel enthusiastic about, they spread the word and pass it on."

Kalin also decided that it wasn't in the best interest of the Etsy brand to pursue traditional media outlet advertising, so he stuck to his idea of making his website seem more like a social media experience by including features such as an Etsy blog, craft videos, community-driven seller groups (known as "street teams"), and a section that focuses on seller tools and articles that highlight shops throughout the website. His strategy worked, because almost 80 percent of members learned of Etsy through a friend.

Learning the markets on Etsy basically boils down to three sections: handmade, vintage, and supplies. Each section has a unique audience, but there is also steep competition. You have to decide which path you want to go down (and you can mix it up all in one shop) and learn to abide by Etsy's rules.

- **Handmade:** Any item that is handcrafted by artisans or designed by them and created in their studio is considered handmade. This includes items that are premade and embellished/altered by the shop owner.
- **Vintage:** Items that are clearly identifiable as twenty years of age or older qualify as vintage. Clothing, home goods, collectibles—anything goes as long as the item was produced more than twenty years ago.
- **Supplies:** Items having the primary purpose of being turned into something else are supplies. Some items can stand alone, but if they are a staple of creating any craft, they are considered to be supplies.

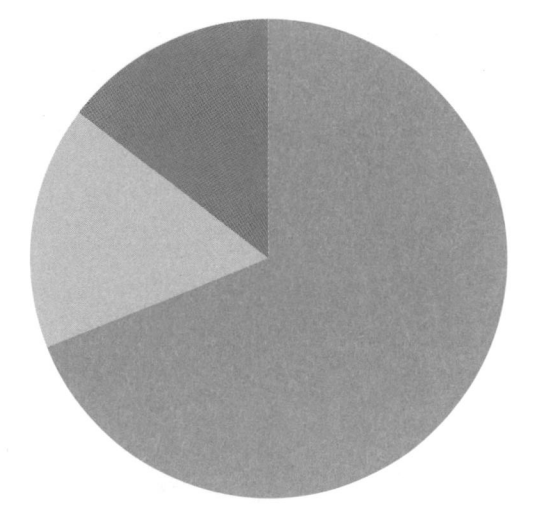

■ Handmade 13,806,948 listings   ■ Vintage 3,306,131 listings   ■ Supplies 2,918,959 listings

Data compiled March 9, 2013

Now that you have a better understanding of the three markets on Etsy, let's look at what makes each one unique.

Welcome to the Handmade Revolution

With more than thirteen million handmade items listed on Etsy at any given time, the numbers alone show that the marketplace is huge. The bad news, of course, is that if you decide to go the handmade route, you'll have to compete with a lot of sellers. The good news is that there are plenty of customers to go around. In the handmade market, the average purchasing customer is a female twenty-four to thirty-five years old who has a little money to splurge and tends to purchase gifts for others more than for herself.

Creating handmade items generally means that the cost of time factors more heavily into the price than the financial cost of the goods themselves. If you love being creative, this may be the market for you.

Etsy's handmade section is broken down into many different subsections, so there is a specific market for anything and everything you can dream of (and even things you never knew existed).

Art

Because "art" is a subjective term, and the website bills itself as a promoter of artists, art is a huge section on Etsy. You can find everything from fine oil paintings to acrylic works, plus pastels, photography, mixed media, and even digital designs throughout the website.

Handbags & Clothing

Most women would agree that you can never have enough handbags or enough clothes, so of course these are popular items, whether they are meticulously created by highly trained designers or simple pouches sewn by the average seamstress. An unknown clothing designer who fills a much-needed void in the market (like plus-size or menswear) can do very well.

Bath & Beauty

Nearly sixty billion dollars was spent on bath and beauty products in 2012 in the United States alone. The beauty of selling lotions, soaps, and beauty products is that customers have to replenish their supplies, so they will come back if they find a product they love. And, because repeat customers are a huge resource for this type of shop, if you have impeccable customer service you'll see your customers over and over again.

Books & 'Zines

Working with digital clients means they could very well be more interested in electronic versions of classic print products such as books, magazines, patterns, and tutorials. The bonus is that once you have created electronic literature, the only additional labor is simply e-mailing your customer the "product." Digital publishing shops are also an excellent way to create continual income on items with little to no overhead.

Candles

Similar to the Bath & Beauty sellers on Etsy, candle sellers have the advantage of selling a product that needs to be repurchased. This creates repeat business. Finding the "perfect" candle scent isn't always easy, but if your products find a loyal following, this type of shop can catch on like wildfire.

Ceramic & Pottery

Artists working in these mediums are finding a following for their wares through Etsy. From classic to contemporary, dishes to sculptures, the styles are diverse and can be very successful.

Children

Anyone who has ever had a child can tell you one thing for sure: Kids use a lot of stuff. Remember how the average purchaser on Etsy is a woman age twenty-four to thirty-five? She probably has little ones, or at least nieces and nephews. Women tend to purchase for their children instead of themselves, so there's an astounding number of buyers for great kid-oriented products.

Edibles

Let them eat cake, and cookies, and scones, and all sorts of yummy things! Gourmet food sellers have the same advantage as Bath & Beauty sellers: Their product is made to be consumed and renewed. If you can think outside the box with an innovative flavor combination, you may find the recipe for success.

Geekery

This is a quirky, yet highly promoted, section on Etsy. If you don't already know what "geekery" is, then you're not the target audience for this popular category. The term is pretty self-explanatory: It caters to all things that the self-proclaimed geek needs. With shirts, pillows, and almost any item imaginable to feed Star Trek fans and the tech-obsessed, this category is filled with things that will appeal to the hearts (or motherboards) of geeks everywhere.

Graphic Design

This is essential in an online world, which is why graphic designers are such an important part of Etsy. Looking to get a shop banner, business cards, or packaging made? Designers with all levels of experience are there to help. Besides just making business-related goods, there are designers with their own digital scrapbook lines, some that specialize in vintage graphic refashioning, and others that gear their goods toward weddings. If you dream of being a digital designer, Etsy is a good place to set up shop.

Housewares

Items in this category are abundant in every form of retail, and Etsy is no different. Pillows, towels, candlesticks, dinnerware, drapery, and even furniture can all be found in the wide range of listings. Every style imaginable is represented and even cataloged in the listings system.

Jewelry

This is the largest of all markets in the handmade area of Etsy. From fine jewelry made by metalsmiths with exquisite gemstones to simple craft-style accessories, there are shops for every type of jewelry maker. These artisans are among the top ten handmade sellers, because shoppers don't own just one necklace or pair of earrings—they love adding multiple accessories to their shopping carts.

Paper Goods

Sellers on Etsy offer everything from tags to gift wrap to gift cards and even journals. Those who cater to the wedding market tend to do very well because they are selling in bulk. The paper goods market is much like that for other disposable goods; paper is a temporary product that needs to be repurchased over and over again.

Pets

Our pets are beloved members of the family, which is why buyers shop for them via Etsy. From dog tags to pet bowls—and even artists who will create beautiful artwork with your pet as the subject—there is something for every pet owner.

Plants

There is a thriving section of sellers that offers everything from unique planters with succulents to seeds of heirloom plants. The only drawback of this section is that not all items can be shipped internationally due to customs laws.

Toys

This is definitely a hopping business during the holiday season, but toys are also a popular seller year-round. Because the typical buyer (remember, she's a twenty-four- to thirty-five-year-old woman) generally has at least one child, she will buy for that child before she buys for herself. Birthdays, Easter, Valentine's Day, even baby showers provide ways for shoppers to show their love through gifts. If you can find something that stands out, selling toys can be a lot of fun.

Wall Decals

These are technically a subsection of the Housewares market, but they are such best-selling items that they need their own section. The removable stickers are easy to ship and relatively inexpensive to make, and they are a hot commodity in home decor. Buyers can change the look of their space in just a few minutes with these precut wall stickers.

Weddings

Your wedding is the one time in life when you splurge to create the big day of your dreams. Brides flock to Etsy to find the perfect pieces to make their wedding day one to remember for a lifetime. Brides can purchase custom-made wedding dresses, rings, and reception goods on Etsy. If you cater to this booming market, you can tap into a big-spending clientele that will buy in bulk.

Finding Your Vintage Vibe

Brush off that notion of vintage sellers with tons of junk—if done properly, vintage shops can thrive! Because the average buyer is fairly young, vintage sellers should think young, too. Items with quirky character, a good worn patina, or an interesting history are all hot sellers in this popular category. With magazines relying heavily on up-cycled and vintage-style projects for content these days, the vintage market is seeing a big comeback.

Vintage sellers can spend large amounts of both time and money to find the very best selections to curate shops that truly attract buyers. This market is about catering to a certain style and then curating a collection of goods that will appeal to the customer who relates to it. Many different items can be combined successfully into one shop, especially if the overall style of the items fits an audience as a whole.

Of course, knowing the best-selling type of items can help you to stock your shop with a winning combination. Top vintage sellers among Etsy overall tend to stick to five main items:

Clothes

Just like in the handmade market, vintage clothes are a huge seller. Top-selling vintage clothes sellers usually have a distinguished look, similar to a clothing designer. Hipster shops, jewelry boutiques, and cowboy boot curators all get rave reviews.

Ephemera

Although they can technically be considered supplies, vintage papers, maps, cards, and other paper goods are huge sellers on Etsy. They are highly marketable to both creators and regular buyers, who might frame them or give them as gifts.

Housewares

Any interior designer will tell you the same thing—vintage goods make a home look better. Mid-century design and modern furniture all sell extremely well on Etsy. The shops that showcase great style can become go-to resources for decorators, magazines, and lovers of all things vintage.

Jewelry

You'll see over and over and over again that jewelry makers rule the roost on Etsy. Vintage jewelry sellers are some of the most popular vintage sellers. Most of them offer bits and parts as supplies as well as wearable pieces.

Supplies

These are always going to be a top seller, as you're among creators. Jewelry supplies sell especially well, which is obviously linked to the fact that there are more listings for jewelry on Etsy than for any other item.

Supplies

Supplies are the heart of Etsy because there is a built-in base of avid crafters and artisans who need supplies to create the things they sell. It's no wonder that supplies are the best-selling commodities on Etsy—each of the top ten overall high sellers is a supply seller. With that huge base also comes a lot of competition, so the key to finding customers is to supply them with your goods at a great price.

Why would anyone buy from a seller instead of from a wholesale site? Wholesalers generally require large purchases, many times larger than a small start-up shop owner can handle from the beginning on his or her own. Supply sellers buy in bulk and then break the purchase into smaller lots for a profit. That smaller price tag can add up to some hefty profits, but it does take more of an initial financial investment than the other two types of shops.

To figure out which supplies sell best, you can basically look at which handmade goods are the top sellers. Catering to those artists is a great idea because the more goods they sell, the more supplies they will need.

Digital Clipart

Images can be used in so many ways, from making items by printing out the graphics to using the pieces in other digital offerings (such as shop banners). Digital art sellers are another section that caters to artists' back-end needs.

Jewelry

Beads, chains, cabochons, rings—basically any item that could be used to create a piece of jewelry is fair game. There isn't a true recipe to finding the best sellers—the jewelry supply shops tend to take a "more is more" mentality and list far more than other types of shops. Some supply shops can have thousands of listings—all of which help to improve their visibility on the site.

Sewing

Sewers are one of the largest segments of crafters in the world. From the average crafter to the advanced shop owner, fabrics, notions, and even patterns all fit into this popular section, which can be quite prosperous.

Scrapbooking

Just like the digital listings, scrapbooking items are extremely popular on Etsy. Scrap-booking is nearly a three-billion-dollar industry—one that has millions of avid customers who regularly replenish their supplies. Digital and actual goods are frequently listed and sell incredibly well.

Time versus Money

Unless you opened this book with a preconceived notion that you wanted to create a certain type of shop, you have a lot to consider. Now that you've seen the three major sections of Etsy, comparing the three basically boils down to one major question: Will your initial investment involve more time or more money?

Financial investments can range from buying supplies to machines, learning a new skill, or even renting a space (but we'll get into that later in the book). Let's say you are starting a handmade shop. You love to sew, you've been sewing for yourself, your family, and your friends for years and years—and you're pretty good at it. You decide to open up a shop making handmade aprons, as you already have a sewing machine, a serger (an overlocking sewing machine used to stitch seams), an iron, scissors, a cutting mat, and all the other basics needed to sew aprons. Your initial financial investment may require only some fabric.

What if you wanted to start a shop for something that you aren't equipped to make? You would have to purchase all the supplies and tools, and you might even need to take a course to learn how to make the item you have in mind. It's not impossible; it's just more expensive.

I originally started my shop with almost no money; instead, the shop relied heavily on my time. In the early days of remodeling our home, I realized we had a huge supply of scrap wood that was too small to use in our renovations but seemed too large to discard. I found a way to turn those scraps into wooden ornaments by cutting them with a jigsaw we already owned and painting them. Within weeks I ran out of scraps and had to purchase more wood for our projects. My shop was literally created out of a scrap pile.

Vintage is similar. You can open a shop with finds from Grandma's attic, but is that the collection you would put out to sell if you were set up with a store where you paid rent, utilities, etc.? If so, that's wonderful! You get to start a shop with a minimal financial investment that relies heavily on your time being used cleaning up the items and photographing, listing, and shipping them (among other time-busters).

If you go the supplies route, your financial investment will most likely be the highest of any type of shop. You will need to purchase very large amounts of supplies from wholesale sources and break them down into lots that your customers will need. Unfortunately, finding the perfect wholesale source isn't always a quick process. It can take hours on end to find that one source for one supply. Your time and money are going to be spent on your stock, but once you have your initial suppliers, you may find that your time shifts to shipping and handling.

Part Time or Full Time?

Sellers come from all walks of life, from those who are fresh out of college and want to start their careers on their terms, to those who just want to sell a little to help pay for a yearly family vacation. There is no right or wrong choice—you just have to choose how much time you want to devote to your shop.

Part-time sellers spend nights and or weekends working on their goods, but they don't look to generate a huge amount of income from them. Most work a day job, either part or full time, and are looking to supplement their earnings either to help pay the bills or to have a little more money for some extra fun. Some sellers are looking only to recoup the amount of money they spend on crafting instead of making a large profit from their pieces.

You should never sell only for the cost of supplies, though, because you will have to pay taxes and fees on that income; then your project can cost more in overhead than the actual supplies cost to begin with. If you're only creating things for fun and not profit, I suggest giving them as gifts or donating to a charity. Selling products at under-market value hurts sellers in the long run, as you are all in the same market.

If you do want to make a profitable part-time income, though, that is possible on Etsy. The majority of shops on the site are run by part-time sellers, some of whom eventually grow their businesses large enough for them to become their full-time job.

Full-time sellers do just that—sell. It is their day job, and many times it is their *only* job. If you have a great product, passion, dedication, and patience, you can successfully run a full-time shop on Etsy. Busy sellers will also tell you that the key is promotion, in whatever form that you find effective. (We'll get into marketing later, in chapter 7.)

Should You Really Open a Shop?

After reading all about what makes Etsy, you're probably asking yourself, "Should I really open a shop?" Only you can answer that question, but here are some things to consider before making the choice to open up:

- **Do I have time?** Running a shop takes more time than just making a few things and putting up listings. You need time to promote your items, work with your customers, package the items for shipping, and handle the paperwork that goes along with owning your own business.
- **Can you make something of value?** With so many amazing sellers on Etsy, you need to make sure your items are quality goods. If you just learned to sew last week, you probably shouldn't be selling sewn items. However, if you have a hobby that you love to do and are well versed in, you can usually translate that into items that are valuable.
- **Are you a "people person"?** Being behind a computer screen doesn't make your buyer any less real than if you had an actual brick-and-mortar store. You need to be able to answer questions, deal with criticism, and work with people to build a thriving business.

If you can answer all of these questions with ease, then you have an idea of whether or not Etsy is right for you.

Nobody tells this to people who are beginners, I wish someone told me. All of us who do creative work, we get into it because we have good taste. But there is this gap. For the first couple years you make stuff, it's just not that good. It's trying to be good, it has potential, but it's not. But your taste, the thing that got you into the game, is still killer. And your taste is why your work disappoints you. A lot of people never get past this phase, they quit. Most people I know who do interesting, creative work went through years of this. We know our work doesn't have this special thing that we want it to have. We all go through this. And if you are just starting out or you are still in this phase, you gotta know it's normal and the most important thing you can do is do a lot of work. Put yourself on a deadline so that every week you will finish one story. It is only by going through a volume of work that you will close that gap, and your work will be as good as your ambitions. And I took longer to figure out how to do this than anyone I've ever met. It's gonna take awhile. It's normal to take awhile. You've just gotta fight your way through.

—Ira Glass

Whether you are selling vintage, supplies, or handmade, when you set up shop on Etsy, you are putting yourself into a handmade world. All the shops are catering to customers who admire creativity and seek it out in their everyday lives. Your job is to learn how to stand out in the sea of other creative minds and find your own place in the market to stake a claim.

When you open up shop in the beginning, it's usually because you have an amazing idea—an idea that may consume you because you see the potential in it, you understand the beauty of it to your very core, and you have an overwhelming passion for it. Those are the best kind of ideas. Once in a great while, a person's vision can be perfect straight out of the gate. Usually it's not. Usually it takes work to transform your idea from the seed that was planted in your mind into a full bloom that bears fruit.

But that passion—the thing that created the idea in the first place—is golden. Learning how to hone that idealistic passion into a marketable good is what sets apart a shop that occasionally gets a sale from one that has constant sales.

There is a series of events that all successful shop owners I know have gone through at some point to land them where they are today. Of course, there are exceptions to this rule, as some people are extraordinarily lucky—but you shouldn't rely on luck. Luck is too tricky to plan on, and it is rarely a component of true success. Also, it may appear from the outside looking in that someone was lucky, but often a huge amount of energy went into that person's seemingly flawless success. These people just don't express the struggles; they tend to concentrate on their craft instead.

Start with an Idea

First, you need an idea. You may find yours through years of training and education, or it may just be a hobby that you have worked on that seems to satisfy an aspect of your creativity. Many times, the main idea may be finding a solution to an everyday problem—and if you have that problem, then you can be sure that others have it, too. In whatever manner you find it, the idea will need to be cultivated and refined so that you can bring it to market.

If you are a sewing whiz, there are multiple directions you can go:

- **Home Decor:** Table runners, pillows, drapes, furniture slipcovers, and aprons are just a few items that can be made by a seamstress.
- **Clothes:** Women's, children's, and men's clothing are all in high demand. Why not take it further? Pet clothes are a huge seller, as are doll clothes.
- **Handbags & Accessories:** Your imagination can go wild coming up with different designs and combinations of fabrics for purses, wallets, shopping bags, zippered pouches, sunglasses cases, iPad/tablet sleeves, phone covers, and tote bags.

- **Toys:** Because there are strict federal (US) laws about creating items for children, cloth toys are a smart way to enter this market. Fabric isn't as regulated as other mediums, so using cloth to make mobiles, plush animals, dolls, and other kid-friendly items is a good choice.

Woodworkers can take the same mentality and spin it to their own individual shop needs:

- **Home Decor:** Many different pieces can be created out of the same basic set of supplies, such as candleholders, wood signs, tables, chairs, ottomans, tags for organizing, boxes, shelves, and even small accessories. A few different paint colors can bring a shop from only a handful of offerings to a plethora of choices with variations of the same objects.
- **Toys:** Just like with fabrics, woodworkers can create an unlimited range of shapes for teethers, dollhouses, cars, tables, toy storage, and puzzles. Classic toys are making a comeback, and woodworkers are taking advantage of that trend on Etsy.
- **Weddings:** Think past the traditional wedding gear and into the realm of what brides might overlook that would help make their big day even more special. Signs that point to the venue are helpful, but if you can create ones that stand out in the crowd, then you may point your business in the right direction, too.

Know that however wonderful your original product is, it will evolve with time. Once you bring it to life, you will find ways to tweak it, so the product that you love gets better and better as time goes on. Your craftsmanship will improve, you may upgrade to higher-end supplies, and your packaging will evolve. Just like everything else that is good in life, your idea will get better with time.

If you are in the beginning of your business, don't dwell too much on revising the product. Work across the board on different aspects of your business simultaneously, so that they all grow and mature along with your business as a whole. The product itself is only a tiny portion of your shop in the entire scope of things. You have to look at the bigger picture to be able to see where you are going.

Envisioning Your Ideal Customer

As you start pulling together your products to open up your shop and before you get too much stock built up, you should consider your customer. Without a good idea of who your ideal customer is, you have no idea who you are selling to. When you do have a grasp on who will be buying your products, decisions like packaging, product descriptions, and even customer service will become easier. If you know who you are selling to, you can cater your approach to their tastes and needs.

You should think of that person through and through, until he or she becomes like an imaginary friend who you know better than anyone else on earth. Your actual customer might not be a 100 percent match, but if you can figure out who you are marketing to, that ideal customer can help you determine if a certain product may or may not be successful.

So how do you find your ideal customer? Start on the most basic concept, then work your way around to the fine details. Don't worry about if your ideal customer fits the typical Etsy audience—this is the place to do what is best for your business.

- **Male or female?** Even though the typical customer on Etsy is a woman, it doesn't matter. There are plenty of men on the site, and shops that cater to them are not nearly as saturated as the ones that cater to women. Men's clothing has a far less competition rate than that of the women's market. Don't think of Etsy as a whole at this point—think of whom your product/idea will benefit more—a man or a woman.

- **How old is your customer?** Knowing their age (even within five years or so) will help you to figure out their generational preferences. Women in their twenties and thirties tend to buy more for children, while women in their fifties and sixties usually buy more for themselves. Younger men seem to have a different sense of style than older men. Understanding their age will also help you to figure out how to gear your packaging, because younger audiences gravitate toward a more modern look, while traditional packaging might appeal to a more mature customer.

- **Married or single?** Although some markets find that this detail will affect them more than others, it's good to think about it. If you are a wedding shop, you want to cater to brides, so you are looking for people in that exact phase of their lives. If your product is geared toward men, remember that the women in their lives are always looking for gifts.
- **Children?** Knowing your target customers can help determine their needs beyond whether or not they need children's items. Busy moms and dads can always use help speeding up their lives with products that keep their families running smoothly. If you sell toys or children's clothes, know that you aren't selling to a three-year-old; you are selling to the mother or father—so market your products accordingly.
- **What type of job do they have?** Supply sellers will be selling primarily to crafters/creators. Artisans who create modern-style briefcases typically gravitate toward business or corporate types. Stay-at-home moms focus most of their attention on their children. If your customer's job can play any role in his or her decision-making process, it's good to think about how.
- **Where do they live?** Although I have lots of customers from urban areas, the suburban and rural areas are also extremely popular, as they have fewer stores that offer unique items. Small towns typically have only a Walmart or Target to offer the bulk of their needs, so shopping online is a great option for those who don't have many local choices. It's also good to think about the exact area, if your product is geared toward a specific type of location. If you are selling beach cottage–style home goods, you are most likely aiming for customers in a coastal region.
- **Besides your shop, where do they buy?** Is your customer the type that purchases her clothes at a mall or a discount big-box store? Even if you don't sell clothes, you can tell a lot about buying habits from where a person fills his or her closet. Shoppers who appreciate quality and will pay for it are a much better fit for the handmade market seller than those who solely look for the cheapest things they can find. High-end shops cater to a certain type of customer—one who is educated, informed, and prepared to spend. Is that the type of customer you'd like to attract? If so, you need to set up your business to cater to that person.

Male or female?	
Age?	
Married or single?	
Children?	
What type of job?	
Where do they live?	
Where do they shop?	

Developing a Business Atmosphere

Thinking through how you want to treat your business from beginning to end is a smart move to make from the very start. Concentrating your efforts on customer service is essential because the old adage is true: "An angry customer tells ten people, but a happy customer tells one." In our digital age, a disgruntled customer can reach hundreds (or even thousands) of people with one simple post on Facebook or a short line on Twitter.

Your business atmosphere will include much more than simple e-mails back and forth with your customer. It includes how you write your listings, the style in which you photograph your products, the care with which you package your items, and even the way you contact customers to let them know when items are shipping.

If you decide up front that you want to be attentive and hands-on with your customers (as much as you can be online), reliable and consistent communication is key. Presenting yourself in a friendly, yet professional, manner will put you far ahead of the competition.

Have you ever been in a shop and needed help, yet no one seemed to be available? Or, if they were available, they had no idea how to help you? We've all had that experience, and it's not a pleasant one. Remember that you know your products unlike anyone else does. You have the ability to share your knowledge and to pinpoint what sets your products apart from the rest of your competition. You can help potential buyers with their questions, but customer service is more than just fielding questions.

When customers purchase something from your shop, Etsy automatically sends them a confirmation e-mail. If you want to go above and beyond with your customer service, send them a quick thank-you note, telling them you got their order and letting them know when it will be shipped. Want to enhance your communication even more? As you pack their order for shipping, let them know it's going in the mail. Those two messages, which take mere seconds to compose and send via Etsy, will stand out in your customers' minds. That small investment of your time into building a relationship with your customers is golden. You have only a small window of time to let them know that you appreciate their patronage. Your appreciation will be an asset to building a loyal and returning customer base.

When you are laying the groundwork for how you'd like to deal with your customers, remember above all else to be yourself. Don't try to be young and modern if you are older and more mature. Be you—and only you. Expand on your strengths and use your natural voice. Building a façade of who you think customers want you to be will only set yourself up for failure down the road, not to mention all the stress of trying to be someone you are not.

Customers know when they are treated with genuine kindness and attention. You can use the same basic wording for multiple transactions with different sales, but always keep your communications with customers authentic and true to who you are.

Let's break down all of the points of contact where you have an opportunity to interact with your customer:

- **Listings:** The vast majority of the time, when a customer comes into your shop, it is through a listing, not via your main shop page. Although there will be more in-depth information about writing listings in chapter 6, you should remember that every single product page will need to have a short introduction to your business. This is often your one chance to draw a potential customer in, to translate that page view into a sale.

- **Main shop page:** When you promote your shop, you will most likely be sending customers to your main shop page. In our social media world, you can never tell when a friend of a friend of a friend who you have never met might end up on your main page. You have room in your shop announcement to make an impression, so take the time to make a good one!

- **When they ask questions:** Customers may ask questions about your listings, even when you have completely described the item in great detail. Some people miss information, or they may ask a question that you had never anticipated in the first place. Either way, this is the time to convey your great customer service by answering promptly and politely.

- **After the purchase:** Once customers make a purchase, they will automatically receive a confirmation e-mail from Etsy about their order. I always send an additional message via the Etsy Conversation system to thank them and let them know the date that their item will ship. It's a simple form letter that I cut and paste from a Word document, changing the relevant information that pertains to their specific order. Sending that extra note takes about thirty seconds, but it helps build a relationship with your customers so that your great communication becomes part of their buying experience.

- **Upon shipping:** After an order has been packaged and is ready to go to the post office, you can send your customers one more message to remind them that their order is going to ship that day. At the end of the final thank-you message, I always add a line that links customers to the store's Facebook page and a link to sign up for our shop e-mail promotions.

- **Handwritten thank-you notes:** Inside each package that I send out, I also include a simple handwritten thank-you note written on the back of my business card. I only write, "Thank you!" and sign my name, just to solidify that their business is appreciated.

- **Leaving feedback:** Etsy's feedback system is not only good for sellers but also instrumental to buyers. When you leave good feedback for

Imitation is suicide.
—*Ralph Waldo Emerson*

your great customers, it is beneficial to you, too. Thank them and tell them that you hope to see them again soon, which helps keep your brand in their memory beyond the original contact.

- **Social media:** If your customers are very, very happy with their whole experience, they will likely follow you on Twitter, Facebook, Pinterest, Google+, Instagram, or whichever social media outlet you frequent. Often, your customers will tag you in photos to share their new purchase, so be sure that you always thank them and promote them as amazing customers. Even large corporations use this strategy, and if it works for them, it will definitely work for you.

- **Newsletters:** If you utilize e-mail marketing, asking your customers to sign up after a purchase is a great way to introduce your new items or sales to customers who have already had the experience of working with you. They know your product quality and appreciate your customer service, so this helps to bring back those crucial repeat customers.

- **Holiday cards:** Some shops that really want to wow their customers keep records of all the mailing addresses of customers who have purchased from them in the past year. At the end of the year, they send out holiday cards (usually postcards) thanking them for helping to make their year successful, and they include a coupon code as a "gift" for their customers. This has a twofold effect: First, it may remind customers who purchased from you early in the year of your brand; second, it gives that customer more incentive to purchase gifts from your shop (which they now love) during the busy holiday season.

Don't feel like you have to make each and every point of contact, but the above examples are some good guidelines. A few of them are vital, especially the listing and home page, because without them you won't have a shop. However, you can determine how hands-on you want to be with your shop by how many times you touch base with your customers.

If your shop grows to the point where you cannot personally keep up with every single point of contact, you can hire a virtual personal assistant to do the e-mailing and other administrative tasks for you. Once you get to that point, your shop will be so successful that you'll be able to hire help.

Figuring out how in touch with your customers you would like to be is a huge portion of developing your business atmosphere. If you decide up front that you want to be on a friendly basis with your clientele versus using an authoritative voice, use all of your points of contact to talk to them one-on-one.

Overall, customers on Etsy typically prefer to talk to you as a person rather than as a business owner. Many of my customers over the years have come back to my shop time and time again thanks to the customer service. They feel like they are reaching out to a friend when they e-mail me.

You have to choose if you want to be highly professional and all business or if you want to be more personal. If you do not want to build up a personal following and just want to sell and ship your wares, then being business-oriented may work best for you and your environment. In the end, you have to choose which direction will get you to your goal.

Customer Service Points of Contact

Create a plan to determine which points of contact you will utilize and how you will put them into action.

Listings (mandatory): _____

_____

Main shop page: _____

_____

Conversations: _____

_____

After purchase: _____

_____

Upon shipping: _____

_____

Thank-you notes: _____

_____

Feedback: _____

_____

Social media: _____

_____

Newsletters: _____

_____

Holiday cards: _____

_____

Writing a Mission Statement

Mission statements can seem a little scary at first. Business experts will tell you to carefully craft two or three sentences that will solidify the intent of your business. It really doesn't have to be that complicated. If your goal is to one day sell off your enterprise to another company, then go for it and construct a statement that reflects the professionalism you are trying to establish. Most handmade sellers need to think only a little to figure out why they do what they do.

All business owners start a business for one reason: to make money. You probably don't want to put that in your mission statement, though. Think about what you hope to provide to your customers, how you want them to feel, and what you want them to think about your business.

Looking at your mission statement from time to time is necessary to make sure your shop stays true to what you wanted it to be from the beginning. Statements may change over time, but they should be broad enough to cover the overall intent of your shop. Think beyond the individual items themselves and look at how you want your customers to view your shop.

You can be more specific, adding in a few key phrases to highlight the best aspects of your business. Craft-oriented business mission statements can be summed up by asking three basic questions:

- **What needs do you wish to fulfill?** Handmade sellers may wish to provide their customers with a unique, well-crafted item. Supply sellers may set out

My mission statement for The Shabby Creek Shop was: "Handmade items add character to a home like nothing else can, and any person on any budget deserves to have a beautiful home."

In my very short mission statement, I included the value of handmade goods, but I also let all customers know that I would work with them, no matter their income. Although I could have made some elitist statement to build up my worth (and prices), I knew my customers to the core. I knew that my blogging audience (which was my original core customer base) was looking to save money. Many of my readers didn't have the skills to do the projects themselves, but they still wanted the handmade touch. I kept my mission statement in line with what they needed.

to give their customers a wide range of competitively priced goods. Vintage sellers may aim to bring old goods back to life with a sense of style. All sellers are fulfilling a need for their customers. What do *you* wish to do?

- **What is the purpose of your business?** Besides just filling a need for an item, how will that item enhance the life of the buyer? Each shop will have a different perspective on this point, but you do need to clarify your overall intent.

- **What is your business philosophy?** Wedding sellers may set out to give every bride a fairy-tale wedding. Vintage sellers may try to be eco-friendly and save the planet by reducing landfill waste. My personal philosophy is, "Every person on any budget deserves a beautiful home." We all have some deep philosophical need that is at the core of our creative hearts. Use yours to connect with your customers.

Writing a Mission Statement

Consider the following questions:

1. What needs does your business wish to fulfill? _____

_____

2. What is the purpose of your business? _____

_____

3. What is your business philosophy? _____

_____

Combine your answers to these questions into one paragraph: _____

_____

_____

_____

_____

_____

Finding the Best Name for Your Business

Most people want to jump the gun and figure out a name for their business first. It is similar to naming a child: You want to call your business-baby something so that you have a point of reference. I understand the logic behind it, but I truly caution you to think about what you want to make, who your customer is, and what kind of business atmosphere you want to have before deciding upon a name.

Your business name is not 100 percent set in stone, but you should carefully consider all your options before securing one. You want to think timelessly but also make a point to keep it somewhat personal. If you choose some off-the-wall name, then you will be asked a million times why you picked that name. Even Etsy itself has spawned many blog entries and website articles pondering the meaning of some made-up word.

Before you start the process of deciding on a name, you need to ask yourself one major question: Do you want to be the owner of a brand, or do you want to be known as a personality/artist? Knowing the difference between the two and choosing your path accordingly will make selecting a name a much easier process. Here's how to compare the two:

- **Owner of a brand:** Individual items are the stars of your shop. You are not looking to be recognized as an artist; you just want to sell your items. If your long-term business goals include selling your business, building a brand is a great route to choose. You will be making people aware of a brand that can be managed by any owner, not just you.
- **Personality/artist:** You are the center of your business, either as the creator or because of your own distinct style. Creating a personality-driven business means that you have no intentions of ever selling to a larger establishment, and you will remain with your company as long as it is functional. Think of Martha Stewart, the perfect example of a business built on the name of its star. Authors do especially well choosing their own name, so if your goal is to write manuals or books to sell online, this is a great way to go.

Deciding on the end goal of your business is a key ingredient in the process of picking your business name. If you are a true artist who wants to be known in your trade, then choosing to use your own personal name in some capacity to represent your business is an excellent choice. There are some great examples out there of this type of business, and if you look at the larger business world you can see how people such as Thomas Kinkade and Kate Spade built mega-businesses on their own name.

Now that you have thought about what kind of business you would like to have, which direction to go, and what type of customer you will serve, you are ready to put on your thinking cap and decide upon your name. Start by listing all of the possible names that relate to your wares. If you intend to sell only pillows, your name should reflect that. Be careful to think through a decision that could cause conflict later, though. If you've been selling pillows for years and doing extremely well with them at trade shows and craft fairs, it might be a safe bet for you to choose a business name that reflects that craft.

Jewelry selling is another area where choosing your name based upon your product is a smart move. It will increase your SEO (search engine optimization, which will be explained in depth in chapter 6) if you have the main keyword that describes your shop within your actual name.

Unless you are choosing your own personal name for your business, keeping the name short and to the point is important for a few reasons.

Memorization

It is a proven fact that the human mind best remembers things in odd groups up to seven. (This is why we have seven digits in our phone numbers.) You don't want your business name to be too long for your customers to remember. In the online world, there is generally a virtual trail that can help your customers find you: They can either bookmark your shop, add you to their favorites on Etsy, or, if they purchase from you, find your shop through their order history. Real life is a little different. Unless your shop name is self-explanatory and easy to remember (like 5 Dollar French Market), the potential customers you meet in real life may have a hard time finding you online.

I simply tell new people I meet to Google "Shabby Creek"—because although both words are common, my business is the largest one online that combines the two words. If I know people personally from my past (such as old friends from high school), I tell them to Google my name, because even if they end up on Facebook, my blog, or my Etsy shop, all of my online sources are interconnected to make my shop easy to find.

Branding

Long-winded brand names can be difficult to turn into a logo, especially a logo that will fit onto any medium. You may have a long, skinny shop banner, which looks beautiful when filled with a long name in a great font. That same long name may be difficult to fit onto a business card, though. If you choose to have round stickers made to enhance your packaging, you could face yet another challenge. Shorter names fit better into tight spaces. Be aware that one word might work best; if not, two or three very short words work well, too.

Readability

Does your name sound like it is spelled? Can your customer instantly pronounce your brand name without question? If not, you're not doomed. Look at Etsy—some pronounce the site name *eat-see,* while others pronounce it the proper way: "Betsy" without the B. Etsy isn't the only company out there that has a confusing name—shoe manufacturer Saucony also had a similar issue. When the company first began mass marketing their shoe line, the brand packaging inside the box included a pronunciation guide (say *sock-a-knee*). It can be fun to play the guessing game, but know that it is harder for your customers to spread the word about your great business if they are not sure how to pronounce your name. Using a made-up word can be effective if you find the right combination of letters that is pronounceable, is memorable, and relays your image properly.

Stellar Seller Tip

I wanted my shop name to reflect our goals, which were (besides making money) to have a creative outlet and express our faith. I asked a bunch of friends and my blog readers to make suggestions. Then we wrote all of them on our huge dry-erase board. (There were more than two hundred suggestions!) Over a period of three days, my family all got into the task of choosing a name. Each person put their initial next to the name they liked best. That narrowed it down to ten favorites. Then it was up to me. I wrote them on a piece of paper and taped it to the bathroom mirror. Over the next few days, I would mark through them one by one until I finally decided on "Shop 24." I liked the simplicity, and the number 24 comes from the verse in Proverbs, "She makes linen garments and sells them, and supplies the merchants with sashes." It was perfect! And it has allowed me to grow over the years.

—*Lisa Pennington, shop24.etsy.com*

Going through the process of finding your own unique name may not be easy, but if you take the time to carefully consider all your options, you will eventually settle on a name that combines all of the elements to truly represent your business in the very best light.

Refining Your Product Line

Once you have found your ideal customer, established a business atmosphere, created a mission statement, and decided on a name for your business, refining your line is the next step in the evolution of your business. The great part is that this happens over time, not before you get started. You can make minor adjustments to some items before adding them to your shop, which is why having a small test group of friends and family can be an asset to your business.

Items that are utilitarian need to be tested before selling so that you can see how well the goods will fare with daily use. If you're selling handbags, make a few of them and give them to your friends. Ask them to use the bags for a few days or weeks and then give you feedback. Does the bag work well for them? Does it need more pockets or better straps? Is it large enough or too big? Ask specific questions, but also let them just tell you what they like and don't like about the bag. Make sure that you choose people who will give you honest, unfiltered opinions. It may hurt at first, but take any feedback as constructive criticism to help you grow your line into a great collection of well-thought-out and tested goods.

Decorative items can be fielded in a different way. If you are making hand-painted signs, ask your mini test group to suggest words or quotes that they love and would display in their own homes. If you are looking to narrow down paint colors to the ones you believe will be the best sellers, go to your local paint store and see which paint chips are chosen the most (i.e., which paint chip slots are empty or nearly empty). Then you will see which colors are hot and which ones are not.

Over time, you will have customers come to you who love your items but want them tweaked to meet their own personal tastes. Often, those small changes can lead you to add that "new" item to your line.

Listening to your customers and taking cues from them to refine and develop your line is often a smart move. Originally, I started my shop to sell hand-painted signs, but over the course of three years, I transformed my shop by adding pillow covers and table runners. Gradually, I added in a few sewn items. As they began to sell better than the wood items in my shop, I eliminated the wood items and added more and more sewn items. My shop changed because I listened to my customer base and refined my line to meet its wants and needs.

If you have a few items that seem to sell better than the other items in your shop, take a look at why those particular items may sell better than the rest. Are they fulfilling a need that your customer has that you don't see? If you sell one hundred items in your shop, there are probably twenty items that sell the most frequently. Look at those items and try to create more items that fill the same needs for your customer that the best-selling items do.

Understanding your customers helps you to decipher their buying patterns and know how to replicate the success of your best-selling items to increase your sales. The more goods you have in your shop that customers need, the better your chances of multiple-item orders and repeat orders.

The key to refining is to take the feedback you receive from your friends, family, and customers and use it to make your items better, but refining also involves looking at your sales patterns to fill your shop with the very best-selling items. Although the shop space on Etsy is virtual, so you have no limit as to how much you can sell, handmade sellers need to avoid overwhelming buyers by putting too much in their shops.

Supply sellers can take the same information and translate it to their businesses, too. Look at which items you sell the most within your shop. Can you add a different color? Can you create bigger lots of the items? Can you add variety packs? Are sellers buying from your shop, or are most of your customers crafters? Studying the buying patterns of your customers can let you know if you need to adjust your lot amounts up or down (or both, if need be).

Once you have your shop established, you'll also need to learn how to grow. All sellers can take advantage of Google Trends to see what's hot in whatever market they are in. A simple search will show the amount of traffic for those keywords compared to the past, and the higher the number, the hotter the item is. Keywords such as "vintage" have a much higher Google Trends rating than the keyword "antiques." If you are looking to expand your market, using Google Trends will help you decide if the time is right for that particular item. You'll learn more about how to maximize your keywords in chapter 6, but learning how to find top trends is especially useful for supply sellers who aren't sure where to expand.

The key is to find what works, then do it again. Weed out what doesn't work, and keep enhancing your shop with what does work. It may seem hard, almost impossible, but if you think back to your customer base and your mission statement, you will eventually be able to construct an entire shop of goods that are exactly what your customers need. This part isn't easy—it takes time, patience, and a lot of thinking outside the box. Once you find what does work and what doesn't, infusing your shop with new items will become easier and easier with time. You just have to fight your way through it.

03 Getting Started

Now you know what Etsy is and have a plan to create a line of products to offer your customers. You understand who your customer is, have a good idea of the direction you want your brand to go, and are ready to open up shop. Congratulations! You've crossed through the barrier that holds most creative minds back—actually opening up shop.

Once you get to this step, it can be rather scary. Opening up shop for a handmade artisan is especially frightening emotionally, because you are allowing others to see into your creative world. You are allowing a bit of your creativity to find a new home. The fear will subside with time, but in the beginning you may find that emotional attachment to your hand-crafted items sneaks up on you. It's normal—expect it. Not everyone has this issue, but creative people have a tendency to be emotional, even forming attachments to their creations.

Supply sellers may not have this same attachment, but vintage sellers might form a similar attachment to the pieces they find. Vintage curators seek out beauty, bring it home, clean it up, and make it usable again. They bring pieces back to life, which takes a lot of creativity in its own right. Most vintage sellers want to hold on to everything, but they understand that letting things go creates more room for other items. Some vintage sellers might use objects for a little while, then sell them to make room for new pieces to love.

But you've decided to make a business out of this. You've chosen to part with the creations or items, so you need to learn all of the intricacies of how the business end will work. Setting up the proper paperwork and purchasing licenses are essential parts of starting your business off on the right foot.

Managing an Office

You will need to find space in which to complete all the necessary paperwork to keep your business running. We'll learn more about the items an office space needs in chapter 4, so for now let's talk about the importance of making time and space for all your office needs. Every shop owner I know hates this part—the paperwork. Creative people can have paint under their fingernails, splinters in their skin, clay on their hands, and fabric strings all over, but doing the paperwork is often considered the real dirty work of owning your own business.

First, you need a schedule. The more often you pencil in time for paperwork, the less time it will take in one sitting.

Managing a Studio

Factoring in studio time is essential, especially when you create things for a living. Even if you are a vintage seller or a supply seller, you will still need to manage the day-to-day operations that keep your business running smoothly. Managing your in-studio time will include scheduling time to fill orders or replace sold stock, creating new items for listings, doing maintenance on any machinery, and replacing your supply inventory.

Studio management will look entirely different depending on what type of shop you run. Vintage sellers will find that their studio time isn't just inside the walls of a room. Most vintage sellers spend weekends at flea markets, yard sales, and vintage shows, as well as doing some old-fashioned picking (as seen on several popular television shows). Vintage sellers have different approaches, but most of their time will not be spent at a worktable. Although most sellers find searching for new items to be the fun part of their job, it is still work and should be approached as such.

Once they have returned to their workspace (hopefully with a fresh batch of amazing finds), vintage sellers will spend their time cleaning and caring for the items before creating listings. Computer time is another large portion of their schedule, because vintage sellers often learn to "go with their gut" or buy what appeals to them aesthetically. If an item looks great and is at a low price point, some sellers will buy it before knowing what it is truly worth. After they have the piece ready to list, they may need to do research to find out the market value of that particular item.

Choosing a Paperwork Schedule

Daily

If you decide to sit down at the end of the day every day and take five or ten minutes to do your accounting, you will never lose half a day to paperwork. This is the most manageable way, but it truly works only for super-organized people. Inputting three or four receipts (or however many the day brings) every afternoon will certainly be the easiest way. If you can train yourself to handle it daily, it will save time in the long run.

Weekly

Setting aside a couple of hours once a week to handle all your bookkeeping is another great option. You're not tied down to a daily chore, and it will probably begin to take less than an hour if you maintain the weekly routine. There will be more to input, but it will most certainly keep you from spending a whole afternoon dealing with paperwork.

Monthly

Bookkeeping monthly can give you a broader look at how your budget is doing, much more so than a daily or weekly scope. Some paperwork needs to be done only once a month, so choosing to do all your paperwork once a month might help you keep it all straight.

Quarterly

Budgeting, purchasing, inventory, etc., all need to be completed at least once a month to ensure that your shop is running smoothly. But there are also quarterly matters to attend to, including paying business taxes, self-employment taxes, and wages for employees (if you have them). The easiest way to remember is to mark a wall calendar with each quarterly deadline and build it into your paperwork schedule.

Yearly

Every year, income taxes must be filed (by April 15 in the United States). I strongly urge you not to let your paperwork pile up to only be completed once a year. Not only will you create a huge headache for yourself, you will also have to pay penalties for those fees and taxes not paid on time quarterly. If you maintain your paperwork throughout the year, tax time will be a breeze for you and your accountant.

Occasionally I might go on a vintage shopping trip and bring home items that I thought would enhance the overall appearance of my shop and add to my collection of handmade goods on Etsy. With very little knowledge of the worth of vintage goods, I was definitely a "go with your gut" buyer. I found a beautiful 1960s vintage typewriter for only two dollars at a local thrift store. I knew that I could definitely resell it to my aqua-obsessed customers, so I picked it up. Before listing, I knew that I had to do research on how to price my item so that I would be able to make the most profit while still maintaining a reasonable price point. I was amazed to see similar items listed in online vintage shops for upward of one hundred dollars. If I hadn't known the worth of the item, I might have sold it for only twenty dollars, robbing myself of all that additional profit.

While vintage sellers are spending their time hunting, cleaning, and researching, supply sellers are all about research and packaging. They research to find the best-selling supplies, then research more to find the perfect place to purchase them. It's an endless spiral of learning what customers need and where to find it for them. After suppliers receive the shipments, they spend even more of their time in the workroom repackaging the items for resale.

Finding the perfect pieces for resale is definitely important, but supply sellers might also think about adding extra effort to the repacking part of their business, too. Because their customers are typically crafters and artisans, the package they send out should be attractive to those people. Some customers may not care about the extra fluff; instead, they want the lower price. If you're not an over-the-top packaging person, then go for those customers who want to save on the details. There are both types of customers out there, but if you spend a little extra time and effort on your packaging, you will find repeat customers. The bare-bones seller may not have the same loyal customer base. You want to sell good products at a good price, then do it over and over again. If you can bring back the customers who need your items and love the extra touches that make yours unique, it will be easier to resell to them in the future.

Handmade sellers run their studios in a completely different fashion from either supply or vintage sellers. They need time to create and lots of it. As a handmade seller, you are probably a creative soul who can lose track of time once you get completely involved in a project. Hours can go by in the blink of an eye. You will need to schedule yourself so that you have time not only to fulfill your current orders, but to work on new items as well.

If handmade sellers have a steady stream of sales, you can easily convince yourself that you do not have time to make new product. Weeks may go by with no new items; then, sales will suddenly seem to dry up. Consistently adding in new items, whether it is daily, weekly, biweekly, or monthly, will help keep your shop moving forward and combat any downtime. Some sellers create an entire line of new goods every season.

Stellar Seller Tip

Artist Jennifer Rizzo launches a large batch of new products with a common theme at one time. Rizzo explains, "Having a theme actually gets me motivated, and helps me focus on what I want to make, and I think I just like the excitement. I do like to add new products along the way after a launch."

—*Jennifer Rizzo, jenniferrizzo.etsy.com*

Developing a schedule of how often you want to produce new items and adding it into your workweek will help to push you creatively, and it will also help you concentrate on the overall movement of your shop. You need to give it fresh energy occasionally so that it will not become stagnant. Imagine walking into a shop that you love, but it has the exact same products available as last time you visited. You may give the shop a few more chances, but if you never find anything new, you will not return very often. Your customers think similarly; they want to see new items. If you offer your customers new products to look at, then they will return to your shop more and more. The more often they look at your shop, the more likely they will be to make a purchase.

All shop owners must make time for different aspects of the actual product time, including creating, cleaning, and packaging—whatever you need to accomplish to get the product ready for your customer. Yes, each shop will have a different schedule, but you need to be aware of everything that must be completed. If you can learn to keep to the schedule you create, then you will find consistency to help maintain your business and help it grow.

Business License: Sole Proprietor, LLC, or Something Else?

As the owner of an Etsy shop, you can choose different forms of business organization, depending upon your needs: a sole proprietorship, general partnership, limited partnership, limited liability company (most commonly called an LLC), or, though unlikely, a trust. Different shops will each have different needs, so you should consider a few things, including limited liability, tax considerations, how many people are investing in the business, how you want to withdraw money from the business, and the cost of forming and maintaining the entity.

CPA James Pennington explains the differences between the options:

> *If legal liability is a concern, an LLC provides limited liability for all owners. The limited partnership offers liability protection for the limited partners. General partners and sole proprietors have unlimited liability.*
>
> *Sole proprietorships, partnerships, and trusts pass their income and deductions through to their owners, who pay tax on their share of the taxable income of the business. Corporations pay income tax on the taxable income of the corporation, but may elect to be taxed as a Subchapter S corporation, which is taxed similarly to a partnership. Limited liability companies sometimes have a choice as to how they are taxed. A single-member LLC is disregarded for federal tax purposes and the owner is taxed on the net income of the business, or it may elect to be taxed as a corporation. A multiple-member LLC is taxed as a partnership unless it elects to be taxed as a corporation. An LLC electing to be taxed as a corporation may further elect to be taxed as a Subchapter S corporation. Further, one must consider how the entity will be taxed for state tax purposes.*

Pennington also explains withdrawing of profits:

> *Regarding withdrawing profits from the business, owners of sole proprietorships, partnerships, and Subchapter S corporations pay tax on all income whether distributed or not. Owners of corporations*

and Subchapter S corporations must take out income in the form of wages, which is subject to payroll taxes. If the owner of a corporation, which has not elected to be a Subchapter S corporation, takes out profits in addition to his or her wages, they are treated as dividends and the corporation and the owner both pay tax on that income.

As for the business license itself, some jurisdictions require business licenses and some do not. It is best to check with your local government to see what steps you need to take to get your business up and running. For more information, visit the Small Business Administration website at www.sba.gov.

Filing for an EIN

Working with websites dealing with financial matters, regardless of how secure they are, you will at some point be required to supply either your Social Security Number (SSN) or an Employer Identification Number (EIN). Because of the sensitivity of a Social Security Number, it is much smarter to apply for an EIN to use on your applications than it is to use your personal SSN.

So what is an EIN? The Employer Identification Number acts like a business version of the Social Security Number. It is assigned by the US government to be the marker for your business. You may not need one, but I believe it is better to be safe than sorry on this issue.

You can apply online for an EIN in a matter of minutes at the Internal Revenue Service website (www.irs.gov). There are also options to apply over the phone, via fax, or through snail mail. The online option is very quick and easy to use, and you will have the number the same day. Once you have the number, you can use it to open a business bank account (or PayPal account), apply for a business license, or complete your tax returns.

Bookkeeping

Your bookkeeping method depends on your choice of business entity, the size and complexity of your business, and your reporting requirements. Very small shops won't need complicated bookkeeping, but larger shops that decide to use an LLC may find they need to keep more detailed records.

A small sole proprietorship can simply keep a running total of income and various categories of expenses, which can be done on a columnar notepad. Keeping all receipts and adding them up, as well as keeping track of your sales, will be the mainstay of your bookkeeping; however, you should also track losses. Losses can range from problems with materials, replacements that are reshipped due to damage, and even promotional discounts you offer.

However, any of the other forms of entity should use a double-entry bookkeeping system that tracks assets, liabilities, income, and expenses, because their federal income tax returns may require that reporting on a balance sheet. The most common system in use is QuickBooks. It is probably also the most user-friendly and cost-effective, but a very small business may get by with simply an Excel spreadsheet.

Aside from just keeping up with profits, losses, and purchases, consider finding a CPA to help you find the maximum number of deductions available. We'll talk more about how to find a good accountant in chapter 8.

Insurance

Your insurance requirements depend on how you run your business and what type of liability exposure you have.

- **General liability:** If you have a physical location where you meet customers, then general liability insurance would protect you from injuries a customer might sustain on your property from a slip and fall or other accident. Even if you do not have a physical location, some Etsy shops need general liability insurance for product reasons. Bath and beauty product makers should certainly have insurance in place because their products are applied to skin, opening up potential liability issues due to negative reactions.
- **Personal liability:** If you run your business out of your home, your homeowner's insurance policy may include personal liability that may cover you for such accidents.
- **Automobile:** If you use your vehicle regularly for your business, you may need commercial automobile coverage if your personal automobile policy excludes accidents that occur in the course of business, such as trips to the post office or craft store.
- **Worker's compensation:** If you have employees, you need to investigate your state's requirements regarding worker's compensation insurance, which covers injury to your employees while they are working.

- **Business interruption:** For more sizable businesses where you depend on the income for your livelihood, you might want to consider a business interruption policy, which would compensate you for times when you cannot conduct business due to a fire, flood, or other disaster.
- **Disability:** If others depend on your income, you should consider disability insurance, which would compensate your family if you were not able to work due to a temporary or permanent disability.
- **Life:** Similarly, if others depend on your income, consider life insurance, which would compensate your family in the event of your death.

04

Outfitting a Home Office Space

Odd how the creative power at once brings the whole universe to order.

—*Virginia Woolf*

Carving out a space to start your creative venture means something different for every type of seller. Because no two artists are alike, no two spaces will be alike. The amount of space you have access to can dictate what direction your business will go, so if you are contending with limited space while trying to plot the direction of your business, you should decide where you will work.

Small spaces shouldn't be a deterrent to growing your business, but if you live in a tiny apartment, it may be hard to have a shop that requires a huge screen printing machine. If your goal is to have your business located entirely at home, you need to recognize how much available space you have at home to devote to your business.

Living in larger homes can give you more flexibility, but it can also lead to greater headaches if your shop starts to invade your living space. Artists who can find a dedicated space for their business needs will be more focused when they are in that space.

What if you don't have room to create? Here are some things to consider:

- **Digital businesses take the least space:** Usually digital designers, pattern/tutorial sellers, or e-book authors can keep all of their goods on a computer. A laptop takes up barely any space, and a desktop takes very little. Add a little room for bookkeeping essentials, and if you can find room for a desk, you can have room for a business. Bonus: You can take your business on the road with you—orders can be filled from any location with a laptop and a wireless connection.

- **Share a studio:** Renting a space outside of your home is an option for those who don't have room to spare. Find another artist who also needs to expand and share the space as a joint venture. You don't have to merge businesses for both of you to use the space to create your items.
- **Rent off-hours spaces:** Food sellers often find success in renting a restaurant kitchen during the off hours of an already established space. This win-win solution helps the restaurant owner make money even when the business is closed, and the food seller automatically has the necessary food licensing requirements in place.
- **Build inventory in batches:** If you can fit your items in your home but it creates chaos for the living space during creative times, set up your work area once and crank out mass amounts of product before returning the room to its intended use. You'll have product sitting on the shelf ready to go, which gives you more time to tend to other aspects of your business during the non-production times.

When you find the space to set up a studio, you need to make the absolute most of it. You're paying for that real estate (in whatever fashion), so you will want to get the utmost out of that investment. The best working space will fulfill all of the needs of your business, which may include things that you don't necessarily think of when putting together a studio.

Get in the Zones

A studio for an Etsy shop will require five main zones: a space to create goods, some room to take care of administrative needs, an area to keep inventory, a place to photograph goods, and a location to pack up items for shipping. You don't have to put it all in one room, but setting up zones for these five important needs will make the process much easier to control from start to finish.

Zone 1: Creative Space

Owning a handmade business means that you have to, well, make stuff. What you make will determine how much room you will need, but you should also look at how much space the supplies you have will cost you in terms of storage.

Supplies should be organized, not just so that you have a neat and tidy room (because creative souls tend to be clutter lovers), but because being organized will

What items do you need to create room inside your studio and/or office space? List each item in the appropriate zone.

Zone 1 — Creative Space: (fabric, sewing machine, thread) _____

_____

_____

Zone 2 — Inventory Area: (all your products)_____

_____

_____

Zone 3 — Photography Space: (camera, tripod, backdrop) _____

_____

_____

Zone 4 — Administrative Area: (computer, paper, file space) _____

_____

_____

Zone 5 — Shipping Area: (boxes, labels, cards)_____

_____

_____

save you time in the long term. If you spend two hours looking for a certain piece of fabric in a chaotic studio, you will be losing two hours of productivity that could translate into a lot of product. Yes, it takes time and effort to get organized. It can be overwhelming, scary, and even exhausting, but the long-term time savings are well worth the short-term time loss during the organizing process.

Once you get organized, putting away everything at the end of the day will take only a few minutes, and your studio will be ready for you when you start up the production process again. Don't fall into the mind-set of "I'm not neat." You don't have to be perfectly neat! You just need to put things in places where you can find them within five seconds instead of grumbling while you search for a lost supply or even buying a new one because you couldn't find the original (which, by the way, will only add to the chaos and clutter).

I've been there, really I have. I am not a neat person by any stretch of the imagination. But once I forced myself to cull out all of the unnecessary items and find a home for the main supplies, my production time went from forty-plus hours a week down to about ten hours a week. I spent two long years working too many hours, just because I was always looking for what I needed.

Supplies can seem to grow really quickly, occupying a bigger and bigger section of your work area if you let them. Creative souls tend to shop in places that are full of inspiration, which is a great thing! But do not get swayed to purchase items you "might" use. You cannot buy your way to success. Only bring items that have a specific purpose into your workspace. Bringing in boxes and bags of random supplies will not inspire you; it will only stress you out by contributing to the clutter. Breaking the buying habit will not only save you time and frustration, but your wallet will thank you, too.

If your business deals with supplies or vintage goods, you may not think about room for supplies, but you will still have items that are essential to your business and supplies that enhance your products. Supply sellers may need to store repackaging materials, such as bags, small boxes, or labels. You may also need tools such as cutters, scissors, etc., to unpack large wholesale lots and break them down into smaller lots for resale. Vintage sellers will find that they may need cleaning supplies or even craft goods (such as paint) to spruce up their wares for selling.

Knowing where you will work and storing all of your items close to your workstation will ultimately make managing your time easier. Running from one end of your home to the other to get simple supplies such as paper towels can be distracting. Leaving your work area not only decreases the actual hands-on time that you have, it also makes it easy to get sidetracked and drawn in another direction while away. Keeping all of your supplies together will help you keep focused and get the job done faster in the long run.

Zone 2: Inventory Area

All of those items you are putting up for sale will have to have a home, so be sure to make room for them. Selling vintage items or supplies means you have the items up front, ready to ship. If your shop has a large inventory, you will need a massive amount of space to store all the items. Handmade sellers can either have items ready to ship, or they can make the original item and then create a replica of that item once it is reordered. Either way, you need to consider some options when choosing the right storage solution.

- **Are items large or small?** Small items can pack away neatly in baskets or bins, but larger items might require shelving to hold them properly. Understanding your product sizing can help you make the most of every square inch of space. Supply sellers can sort out their goods into sellable packages and then put them into sorted bins so they are ready to pack upon purchase. Vintage sellers may have better luck with shelf systems that will allow them to find their goods at a glance.
- **Are items fragile or sturdy?** Breakable items cannot be stacked or easily moved around as much as lighter and more durable products can be. Consider putting precautions in place for delicate goods. One-of-a-kind pieces can be wrapped for shipping and then tagged with a Post-it for identification to expedite orders when purchased.
- **Are items temperature sensitive?** Food vendors or bath and beauty sellers may find extreme hot or cold situations alter the integrity of their goods. If you need temperature control for your products to be stored properly, factor that into your plans for organization.
- **Are items available in multiple sizes?** Items can be tagged while they are being prepared for storage either individually or by labeling the appropriate container. Sending a size 2 shirt to someone who needs a size 12 isn't a great way to keep customers happy. Keep all your sizes separated to streamline shipping.

Zone 3: Photography Space

Online businesses thrive on visual cues. Without photos you cannot sell physical goods. Most sellers will tell you that they hate the photography process. Finding a good location that works well with the natural light in your area will be an asset when setting up a space for taking your photos.

Although we will go into more detail in chapter 6 on the art of photographing items, now we'll talk about finding a dedicated space with the sole purpose of always being ready for photographs. Sellers who dread the photography part of running a shop generally despise it because setting up for photos can be a nightmare. However, if you have a corner or area that is always clean and set up, ready for a photo at a moment's notice, then you will find that it is much easier.

Once you understand the lighting in your home, through some trial and error you will be able to find the perfect time and location to take product photos on a regular basis. That area may not even be in your studio, but wherever it is, if you keep it photo shoot–ready at all times, you will not dread taking photos.

Most of my shop consists of pillows, which looked perfect sitting in the corner of my couch. One small corner of my sofa and the side table next to it were the only parts of my entire living room shown in the photos. The rest of the room could be a wreck, and even the other half of the sofa could be covered in a clean pile of laundry, but that never showed in the photos.

Only think about what you need to see inside the frame of the photograph. If your items are larger, then you will need more room, but most small items can be shot in a very tight space. Carving out that small space inside your studio (or elsewhere in your home) will make your photography shoots a breeze. Just pop your item in place, take your photos, and then move on to the next item.

While you are considering the photography space, also think about the equipment needs. Do you have a tripod? Do you have extra lenses? Is there additional lighting equipment? Make sure you have a place to put all of the accessories so you can find them and put them to use quickly.

Stellar Seller Tip

If you put items up in a collection versus putting them up as they are created, you might think about setting up photos with a theme. Artist Jennifer Rizzo explains her process on creating a mood-inspired setting: "Before I shoot a lookbook, I have a general theme in mind and I base all of my staging on what I want to show in that theme. It helps focus things. It's important to use a similar location (idea) so everything goes together and relates. For instance, shooting in the middle of a field one minute and in an office building the next makes no sense in mixing indoor and outdoor shots, but next to an old barn (outdoors) and on some old barn wood (indoors) does and seems cohesive."

—Jennifer Rizzo, jenniferrizzo.etsy.com

Zone 4: Administrative Area

If you are running an online shop, a computer is a must. You are going to be on the computer more than you'd like. You will have to list items, contact customers, promote yourself via social media, keep inventory, and do all bookkeeping. Besides the logistics of running a shop, you will also need room to spread out a bit to do work on several different levels.

- **Lighting:** Editing photos for uploading requires only the room to house your computer and camera, but lighting can be essential to editing those photos correctly. Make sure that your area is well lit to provide the best environment for editing photos to the proper exposure.
- **Filing:** Sales receipts, invoices, and other business documents will need to be organized. A simple filing cabinet or a file box with hanging folders can be a great solution for a tight space. My method of choice is to use manila envelopes, one for each month. They all go into a basket on a shelf, easy to find if I need them and sorted enough to make bookkeeping a breeze.
- **Printer:** Working with a computer almost always means that you'll need a printer. Try to get a printer with a scanner built in, because you may need to scan in receipts or paperwork occasionally. Choosing an all-in-one printer, scanner, and copy machine gives you three functions while taking up only one space.
- **Pen and paper:** Desktop basics such as pen and paper may seem a little outdated, but keeping lists is a good way to keep yourself on track and productive. Having these simple tools at your fingertips is essential for taking phone messages, writing to-do lists, and keeping track of supplies you may need to purchase.
- **Reference books:** Having a few books on your shelf will come in handy, too. Besides this one (of course), you may also find basic writing reference books such as a dictionary or thesaurus handy. You can use online resources, but having an actual book in hand is usually more inspiring than spending even more time glued to the computer screen.
- **Phone:** You will also need room for a phone. It doesn't have to be a traditional house phone, because in this age most people have a cell phone glued to their hands. Just be sure that you have an outside line of communication other than your computer, and you'll be set.

Zone 5: Shipping Area

Physical goods will need to be shipped or delivered in some manner. You can pack up your orders for shipping on the same worktable where you create your products. You still need to carve out some room to organize packing supplies, though.

Depending on the delivery service you use and the type of product you sell, your supplies will vary. Before you decide to sell an item, you need to think about how you will ship it, what will it take to secure that item during transit, and what you will need to make that happen.

Here is a short list of some supplies that you may find valuable for shipping:

- **Boxes:** Free boxes are available for USPS Priority shipping, but you will need to purchase or find any other box. Most box sellers offer discounts on bulk orders, so think ahead if you are purchasing five hundred boxes at once. You'll need a place to store a few for the moment and probably another area to keep the bulk of them. If you need multiple sizes, you may need more than one area to keep them organized.
- **Envelopes:** Very small, unbreakable items can fit inside a standard envelope, but manila envelopes can hold a lot of items that can be shipped flat. I've mailed table runners and pillow covers in this type of packaging for years. Bubble envelopes, which are perfect for small items that may need a little padding but not a lot, are also available.
- **Bubble wrap:** Anything breakable needs bubble wrap, but even if an item is just a tiny bit fragile, you may want to consider adding this to your shipping supplies just in case. Large rolls of bubble wrap are cheaper by the foot than small rolls, but they also take up more space.
- **Tissue paper:** Gift wrap–style tissue paper adds a boutique feel to orders, showing your customers that you took the time to carefully wrap their goods with care. Tissue paper seems to go very quickly, so stock up to keep reorders at a minimum.
- **Branded stickers or labels:** If you are wrapping up orders in tissue or bubble wrap (or both), use your logo on stickers to continue your branding. The more customers see your name, the better they will remember it. Stickers are typically tiny, so you won't need a ton of space, but they make a big impact on your customers.

- **Ribbon or twine:** Tying a ribbon to a package adds another layer of beauty, but if you color-coordinate it with your brand, it can be a small touch that your customers remember fondly. There's a reason that Tiffany & Co. always includes a white ribbon on its boxes—you always remember it.
- **Packing tape:** Everything should be taped. Even boxes or envelopes that come with pre-glued sealers should have the added security measure of packing tape. I even tape both ends of manila envelopes to be sure the factory-sealed edge doesn't budge. If you are using a large tape gun (helpful for really large boxes), make sure you have a place to keep it handy.
- **Tags:** If your item needs care instructions, take the opportunity to put the instructions on one side and your logo or contact information on the other side. When you attach it to the item, it will be another level of branding.
- **Business cards:** Including a business card with every order helps to keep your brand fresh in your customer's mind. Shoppers who buy online often may even forget where the item came from without a reminder inside the package.
- **Mailing labels:** Your package is going to need to get to the customer, and you'll need to address the label to ensure that it gets there safely. Hand-addressing packages adds an additional "handmade" touch, although printing ones from the computer contributes to accuracy.
- **Mailing stamp:** Branded rubber stamps with self-inking pads can be ordered at any office supply store for around ten dollars. It's a small investment that can save you the hassle of writing your own address over and over on mailing labels.
- **Postal scales:** Some sellers prefer to pay their shipping fees online and let their postal delivery person pick up the packages at their door. If you want the convenience of shipping from home, you will need a scale.

This is not an exhaustive list, so if there is something extra that you want to bring to the table, go for it! It's your business and your brand, so if you want to add confetti to your packages, add it to your list. Just consider which products are there for practical purposes and which ones are for beautifying your items.

If your budget is slim when you first start your business, then only bring in the essentials. As you grow, if you'd like to personalize your packages more, just think about how you will incorporate them into your space when adding them to your studio supply list.

The Importance of Staying Organized

Creating space for all the functions of your studio and office will help you streamline your business and make the most of the time you spend working. Knowing where everything should go will help keep your creative business from taking over your home. It can—and will—if you let it.

Until I had a full-tilt emotional breakdown due to the overwhelming amount of stuff that had accumulated throughout our entire home, we lived in creative chaos. Originally I worked from my kitchen table, and within a few months my living room had boxes, baskets, and containers full of supplies. My dining room had been taken over with piles of stuff that seemed to multiply overnight. It was only after deciding to clear out all the unnecessary supplies, get rid of anything I didn't absolutely need, and find a proper home for items I needed daily that I could manage my time properly to bring my business to its full potential.

> Life is too complicated not to be orderly.
> —Martha Stewart

If you're working in a similar environment, you'll find there are multiple benefits to being organized.

- **Time benefits:** You'll be able to make items in the least amount of time possible, because you won't search for lost items anymore. Increasing your productivity level will increase the volume of goods you can create, which in turn can increase your revenue.
- **Calmer atmosphere:** After you spend half an hour looking for something, frustration tends to take its toll. Eliminating frustration is only one part of the calming effect. Not having piles of clutter everywhere will also calm your mind, helping you to enjoy the task at hand rather than grumbling about the stuff that makes you crazy.
- **Financial perks:** Besides the benefit of increased volume, you will no longer buy duplicates of items you cannot find. If you give up in desperation and buy a new tool because you cannot find your old one in the clutter, you're wasting money. Taking the time to put it all away can save you money and make you money.

Being organized isn't always easy for the creative person. Sometimes you'll find that you just can't concentrate long enough to get through it. Remember, I've been there. It took me about six months total to get my workspace from chaotic to organized. If you're just starting out, please consider putting systems in place from the very beginning of your business.

Knowing what you need, culling out what you don't, and finding a place to put it all away are all smart business moves. Think of large warehouses and how organized they are. They are set up for maximum efficiency, for both space and profitability. Take cues from those large businesses and bring them down to your scale as you set up your workspace. You'll find the benefits will far outweigh the time investment.

05

Every Business Needs a Plan

Boring as it may be, every business needs some sort of plan. Think about going on your once-in-a-lifetime dream vacation. You need to choose a location, figure out how you'll get there, and decide what you'll do when you get to your dream spot. Your business is your dream. You need to think about where you want to take your dream, carve out a path to get there, and work toward your goals to get where you need to be.

Starting a shop without any plans whatsoever means that you don't really care if it is successful. And you want to be successful, right? Then you have to determine what success means to you. Success is a very open concept. Every person has a different goal in mind when he or she opens up a shop. Some sellers want only to recoup the cost of crafting to feed their hobby. Others may want to make a little extra spending money. Maybe your goal is to make the extra funds so you can take that once-in-a-lifetime dream vacation. Or your ultimate goal may be to make your shop your full-time income. There is no right or wrong answer—only the goal that is right for you.

Ready? Set? Goals!

Once you determine why you want to sell and what level you'd like to reach in terms of financial success, you can begin to create a path that will lead you to where you want to go. To get there you're going to need to set some goals—on paper, on purpose. Think of it as the map to get from where you are to where you want to be.

Breaking down your course of action into smaller goals will help you to focus on one level at a time, going up your own ladder of success. Once you plan out where you are going and how you will get there, you will only have to focus on the next goal on your agenda, not the overwhelming big goal that seems too far away to grasp. You can't get from A to Z without going through the whole alphabet, and you can't get from where you are now to where you want to be without creating the plan of action that will lay out the course you need to follow.

Setting up a five-year plan is the first part of making your business all you want it to be. It doesn't have to be a world domination scheme, but you need to know what you would like to accomplish in your business.

My Path to Success

When I opened my shop, my goal was to quit my day job. My intention was to replace half the income I was earning as a journalist at a small local newspaper. I figured if I didn't pay for gas back and forth to work, lunches with coworkers, nicer clothes for working with the public, and take-out dinners instead of cooked meals at home, half my income would be enough to make it possible for me to have my own business at home to be more available for our children. Within six months of opening my shop, I reached that goal.

One day, after I had started working on my shop full time, I had a small thought: Could I ever make enough product to sell one hundred dollars a day? I doubted that it was possible but tried to figure out how to make it happen. Within a few weeks, not only was I producing well more than one hundred dollars a day in merchandise, it was also selling. My tiny thought, which I believed was a too-big dream, became reality. After a few months of filling orders at that rate, I found a groove where I could produce even more product every day, so I decided to push myself to sell $150 a day. That number really scared me. It was half my former weekly day job paycheck, which was my goal each week—and I wanted to sell that much a *day*. But, just like before, within weeks I had reached my goal of selling $150 in product a day.

Little by little, I increased my goal, like dipping my feet into an icy pool. Each increment scared me a little, but I worked until I figured out how to make it happen. I made my goals so that I could meet them every day. Some days I more than met my goal; others I fell a little short. Eventually I began looking at a week as my increment, not just one day. I'd set a weekly sales goal and then mentally note how much I needed to sell a day to reach that goal. Some days I might sell $1,500 in product, while others would only bring in $200 in sales. I looked at the week as an average, not just each day.

After a few months of setting weekly goals, I began to set monthly goals so that the weeks averaged out. I would figure out my weekly goals by taking my previous sales, finding an average, and adding 25 percent for a goal to grow. Every time I reached a goal, I created a new one. If I reached the goal in just a couple of weeks, then I'd reevaluate and make a new goal. I reached some goals faster than others. The point wasn't to check off a box on a to-do list; the point of having goals is to push you to grow to where you want to be.

My goals weren't big enough in the beginning. If I had pushed myself harder, I might have gone even further than I did. Goals aren't unattainable obstacles that lead you to frustration; they keep you inspired and on track so that you know where you are going and how to get there. Just don't sell yourself short like I did at first.

Creating a Five-Year Plan

In your absolute wildest dreams, where do you want to be in five years? Be realistic, but think past your immediate needs. Do you still want to be running a shop on a daily basis? Would you like to be able to sell your business to reinvest the money elsewhere? No one can answer this question but you. You know your ultimate goal better than anyone else. When you determine how far you want to take your business in the next five years, then you can break down the plan into yearly goals, monthly goals, weekly goals, and even daily goals.

> A goal properly set is halfway reached.
> —*Zig Ziglar*

Setting Sales Goals

Once you have developed a sense of how far you want your business to go, you need to come up with a figure of how much you would like to sell to get to your profit goals. Use the five-year plan and work backwards to make yourself a timeline that can be your guide. For this example we'll use sales as our guide to put together our plan, with an overall five-year goal of achieving $100,000 per year in product sales (not profit).

- **Break it down to the day:** Selling $100,000 a year in product means that a business has to achieve $8,333 in sales a month. When it is broken down to the weekly total, you will arrive at $1,923. Breaking it down even further, the daily sales goal would be $274.

- **Year one:** If your shop is starting from zero, a good rate of growth would be 20 percent of your overall goal each year, adding as the years go by. In the first year you would need to set a goal of $20,000: monthly sales of $1,667; $385 a week; or $55 a day. Depending upon the type of items sold, this could mean one sale a day or twenty.
- **Year two:** At the 20 percent growth rate, the second-year sales goal would be $40,000, which can be broken down into a monthly goal of $3,333, with a weekly goal of $769 and a daily goal of $110.
- **Year three:** Adding another 20 percent of the original five-year goal will bring the sales goal for the end of year three to $60,000. The monthly sales goal would be $5,000, with a weekly goal of $1,154 and a daily goal of $164.
- **Year four:** Another year adds another 20 percent in our slow and steady scenario. The year-four sales goal would be $80,000, which breaks down to $6,667 a month; $1,538 a week; or $219 a day.
- **Year five:** If your business stays on course for the entire five years, this year will be the $100,000 year. A shop at that level would need to sell $8,333 a month; $1,923 a week; or $274 a day.

Those are really just a bunch of numbers. Don't let them guide you, unless your five-year plan is to have $100,000 in sales. (And if that is your goal, go for it!) Putting together a numeric scenario will help you to construct a business that is set up for success. To get to each of those markers year by year, you will need to think about what you can actually do to obtain the sales to get those numbers.

Profit versus Sales

Sales is the amount of product sold in a day, before taxes, administrative fees, or supplies are added in.

Profit is the actual amount of money made after all fees and so forth have been deducted from the sales total.

Determining Prices

Seeing sales numbers as a whole can be somewhat misleading because sales and profits are not equal in any business. A handmade business doesn't employ the same logic as a supply or vintage business. All sellers have to factor in three major components to determine the perfect price: financial investment in the product, fees and costs of business administration, and time investment.

Financial investment in your product includes all money spent directly or indirectly as part of the overall creation of the item, including:

- **Supplies:** Every ounce of paint, inch of string, and milligram of metal adds to the price of your product. Even a "dab of glue" or "bit of glitter" should be factored into your price because you are purchasing that material to create your products.
- **Tools:** Paintbrushes wear out, sewing machines require needles, and torches take gas. Every tool you use requires maintenance or replacement at some point in time. Including tiny increments of that cost in every item will provide the necessary money when the time comes.
- **Packaging material:** After your item is made and sold, you'll need to purchase the goods to pack and ship it properly. All of the costs of those materials should be added to your price, either in the item price or in the shipping price.

There is a fee attached to every item you sell on Etsy. The cost of doing business goes beyond paying an Etsy bill each month. Business cards, marketing essentials, and office supplies all have to be paid for out of the money that your business makes.

- **Etsy fees:** Any time you add a new item to your Etsy shop, you have 20 cents added to your Etsy bill. If you choose to renew an item, you'll also pay an additional 20 cents. When an item sells, 3.5 percent of the sales price (minus shipping) will also be added to your bill. All of those fees can add up to be a hefty amount, so make sure that you are aware of all of the fees associated with selling on Etsy and factor them into your price.
- **Payment processing:** In the initial setup of your shop, you are given several different options for collecting money from your sales. Each of these comes with a different fee. Most of the options involve a transaction fee plus a percentage of the sale price.

- **Branding essentials:** Account for any business cards, postcards, or other promotional items you need to buy for your business in your prices. This can also include paying artists for graphic designs or hiring consultants to help you increase sales. Any expenses that help to promote your shop as a whole should be considered.

- **Marketing budget:** Although there are many ways to promote yourself online successfully for free (and I'll share tons of great ways in chapter 7), at some point you may decide that purchasing advertising is the next step in promoting your shop. Ads, whether they are print or online, should be factored into your overall item cost.

- **Office supplies:** Ink, paper, staples, tape, and other office essentials that you use solely for business purposes have to be covered. You may also find that you need to purchase photo editing or bookkeeping software, too. If you use it for your business, you should keep it in mind.

- **Office equipment:** A decent computer is a must for running an online business. In addition to your computer, you'll also need a digital camera, although it is not necessary to have a top-of-the-line DSLR (digital single-lens reflex) one. You may find other equipment that you cannot operate without, but those two items are a must for running an online shop. Keep in mind that computers do break and may need repairs—I've been through three laptops in four years. Cameras may need new lenses, repairs, or even replacement with time.

Many of these items should not have a huge impact on the cost of every item, but do add in some business administration fees to the overall cost of your product so that you can maintain this end of your business, too.

Time

Where do sellers spend their time? Each type of seller needs to think of the time they spend in different ways.

Handmade sellers spend their time:

- **Developing a product:** Hours, days, or even weeks can go into designing a product and perfecting the process of making it. Fine artists can spend years in college becoming well educated in the craft of their choice. Besides education, a handmade seller has to dream up a concept, figure out how to make the item, and then find the best and most efficient way to create that item. Some items, such as oil paintings, are one of a kind, while others can be mass-produced a hundred times using the same process.

■ **Purchasing supplies:** You may be able to take a fifteen-minute trip to buy your supplies three blocks away, while a seller in a rural setting may spend two hours driving to the craft store. Even if a seller decides to shop online for supplies, finding the correct item and purchasing it from a website is time spent.

■ **Creating the product:** Unless you are creating unique pieces, once you have perfected the item, you will need time to create the product to be sold. This is the time spent that most sellers consider when they are setting the prices of their goods.

Vintage sellers spend their time:

■ **Shopping for inventory:** Hitting flea markets, yard sales, and auctions may be your idea of the ultimate weekend getaway, but if you are selling your finds, the time you spend finding the perfect pieces should be reflected in your price.

■ **Cleaning and repairing items:** Secondhand finds always require cleaning. It may take five minutes or five hours, but you will have to spruce it up a bit before your item is market ready. What if it needs a fresh coat of paint or some new fabric? The time you spend on that process should be part of your product price.

Supply sellers spend their time:

■ **Finding the best sources:** Supply sellers are in the business of having the most desirable products at the best prices. Anyone who sells supplies will tell you that no matter how amazing your shop is, if customers can get the same goods at a lower price somewhere else, that's exactly where they'll shop. Supplies do not have the luxury of being unique or original—they're typically sold in dozens (if not hundreds) of other shops around the web. For supply sellers to have the best price, they have to find the best price. Researching endlessly to find the perfect wholesale source is crucial.

■ **Breaking down lots:** A supply seller's main job is to purchase mass quantities of goods and break them down into sellable amounts. When you get a shipment of your products, you have to sort them, package them in lot amounts for your shop, and then organize them for easy packing.

In addition to the individual needs of the different types of shops, all sellers spend time on the following:

- **Customer service:** Remember when we discussed all the points of contact for your customer service in chapter 2? All of the time you spend working with your customers is part of your work—and you should always be paid for your work.
- **Photography:** Selling online means that you need photos. You have to take the time to set up products for photography, then edit those photos and get them ready to add to your listings. For shops that sell unique items (including vintage sellers), the cost of photography is greater than for shops who use the same photographs multiple times to sell the same items repeatedly.
- **Listings:** There's a lot to the listing process (which will be described in great detail in chapter 6), but the bottom line is that every item needs to have a listing for customers to purchase it. As is the case with photography, one-of-a-kind items will have a bigger price adjustment for listing time than those that are sold multiple times.
- **Marketing:** Customers can't buy a product unless you help them find it. Marketing your product so that people find your shop can take the most time of the entire process.
- **Packaging:** If you sell a tangible item, you will need to pack it for shipping. Between coordinating the items for the order, wrapping, tagging, writing thank-you notes, creating a shipping label, and taking an item to the post office, you may spend more time packing an order than you did making the item.

Yes, there's a lot of time spent on an item, all of which should be factored into your prices. Keeping track of all that time spent is crucial to making sure that your prices are exactly what they should be.

Retail versus Wholesale

So how do you charge for that time? You have to know what your time is worth. More important, you need to consider if you plan on selling your items wholesale or if you want to keep your business at the retail level.

Perks of Retail

You, and only you, sell your goods. You know your goods better than anyone else, so most likely the very best salesperson for your product is you. By strictly choosing retail, you don't ever have to apply discounts to items in your shop (unless you choose to do so). Most Etsy sellers charge retail, but occasionally sellers find they have better luck selling wholesale to shops if the nature of their product requires the customer to touch or smell it to make the sale, which isn't possible in an online shop (as with bath and beauty products or candles).

Perks of Wholesale

Sellers who decide to open up their businesses to accommodate wholesale orders may find that they make a larger amount of money in one sale. Major clients may need thousands of a given item, though, so be sure that you can handle the workload. If you can, then offering wholesale prices can open up your business to an entirely new set of customers.

Why do you need to consider the retail versus wholesale argument when working on pricing? Because if you intend to sell your goods wholesale, you will have to provide a hefty discount on your products so that other shop owners can purchase your products and then turn around and sell them for a profit.

After you take all of the above information into consideration, you can arrive at your price with a formula that will encompass all three of the factors:

Price of supplies + cost of labor + administrative overhead = wholesale price

Wholesale price x 2 = retail price

Seasonal Sales Cycles

Three months can make a huge difference in business. It may seem like a short time span, but if you implement big decisions that take a while to bloom, then it can be crucial to your business. For instance, Christmas items really should be listed in

August—a full quarter of a year before the actual season on the calendar. If you wait too long, you will miss sales during the busiest time of year. You need to plan ahead, especially for the holiday season.

Customers need to purchase seasonal items long before the actual holiday. Before they can purchase your item, you have to design, create, refine, produce, photograph, list, and promote your items. That's a lot of work! If you have set quarterly goals that address these seasonal issues before they are upon you, the opportunity to capitalize on those sales will not pass you by. I've never heard a handmade owner complaining that he or she started planning for the super-busy Christmas shopping season too early; however, almost every one I've ever worked with wished he or she had planned earlier.

Don't get caught up in the trap of producing only holiday-related items, because the rest of your sales can suffer if you do. Just make sure that you are aware of the best-selling holiday seasons:

- **Valentine's Day:** Jewelry, bath and beauty, and chocolate sellers do very well during this love-filled holiday season. Many sellers start listing their Valentine's Day items the day after Christmas.
- **Easter:** Sellers of home decor, children's items, clothing, accessories, jewelry, and confections can all make sales during the Easter season. Spring is typically a longer season than most holidays, so it can be very beneficial to gear your items toward the spring season rather than the true Easter holiday.

- **Fourth of July:** Party supplies, home decor, outdoor entertaining, and clothes all sell well during the patriotic holiday season. There are international holidays throughout the year, but as much as 70 percent of items sold on Etsy are shipped within the United States, so gearing items toward the Fourth of July holiday is a safe bet.

- **Back to school:** It's not really a holiday, but it is a hot selling season! Bags, books, clothes, and any other items geared toward pre-K through college kids are popular during this traditional shopping season. If you can supply students with some unique essentials, your shop can move to the head of the class.

- **Halloween:** Rare and creepy items are a gold mine during the Halloween season. Vintage sellers who can find just the right scary or odd pieces may be able to market them to people who love this spooky holiday. Clothing shops often sell costumes at this time of year, after the summer clothes season but before Christmas shopping is in full swing.

- **Thanksgiving:** Home goods are popular during this time, including table runners, place mats, pottery dishes, and centerpieces. Customers love anything that will help them set the perfect table at this time of year.

- **Christmas:** This is the biggest season of the year, hands down. Not only are consumers decorating their own homes for the big day, they are also buying gifts for all their loved ones. No matter what you sell, if it can be a decoration or a gift of some sort, you can find big sales numbers during this time of year. Some sellers make as much as 50 percent of their yearly income in the two months leading up to Christmas.

Writing a Business Plan

Because no two businesses are alike, no two business plans will be alike. Funding a business out of your own pocket means that you do not need an extensive business plan for a funding proposal, but having one will help you establish your overall plan—on paper, on purpose.

Just like every aspect of a creative business, you may find that you do not need to address your business plan using the traditional mold; instead, you can alter it to meet your needs. Traditional business plans consist of the following main parts:

- **Executive summary:** Explaining the broad overview of your business will help define the purpose. A short summary that is specific and to the point is all you need. Be sure to include your business name, address, and other vital information, such as hours of operation.

- **Market analysis:** Show that you have thoroughly researched the other sellers in your niche and understand the market and the products offered by your competition. How are your products and/or services better than your competition? Outline how your product compares to the others in your market.

- **Marketing and sales:** Understanding your sales structure, including pricing yourself for success, is highlighted in this section. You will also include how you plan to market your business, either through self-promotion, purchased advertising, or both. Sharing your plan to get sales and grow your business with a goal oriented–plan is an asset.

- **Products summary:** Explain your product in enough detail to give the goods value. Compare how your items are better than those of your competition and compare their differences.

For more detailed information on writing a business plan, visit the Small Business Administration website (www.sba.gov).

Writing a Business Plan

Put together an outline for your business plan. Your actual plan will most likely be several pages long.

Executive summary: _____

_____

_____

Market analysis: _____

_____

_____

Marketing and sales: _____

_____

_____

Products summary: _____

_____

_____

Finding Capital

The beautiful thing about starting a handmade business is that you can begin where you are, on a cash-only basis that requires minimal investment. I highly recommend growing your business only at the rate that you can afford and not going into debt to build your business.

Occasionally you may come to a point in your business where you are faced with a massive retail business who wants to carry your goods, or you might need to purchase an expensive piece of equipment to make your business grow. Personally, I would probably decline the opportunity, even if it was a game-changing proposition, because debt equals risk. Keeping your business in a low- or no-risk position makes it less likely to fail. But if you find yourself in the fortunate position to be able to handle these types of decisions, carefully weigh the pros and cons.

Taking a loan out from a traditional institution will require putting together a fully thought-out business plan and a financial proposal. More help with those can also be found on the Small Business Administration website (www.sba.gov).

06 | The Ins and Outs of Etsy

The next two chapters of this book are the longest for a good reason: They are the most important to the success of an Etsy shop. If you plan on reading only bits and pieces of this book to help improve your sales, these two chapters will mean more to growing your shop and creating sales for your business than any other part of the book. Learning how to effectively set up your shop and create listings for your items is crucial to sales. A good listing doesn't need to be perfect. The most important time you can spend, besides perfecting your products, is spent understanding the key components of what makes up an enticing listing and learning how to get it seen by search engines (including Etsy's internal search system).

Before you start reading this chapter and get overwhelmed by all of the things that you can do to improve your listings, just know that you can start with one or two of them, then work your way through all the steps until you are operating at a manageable pace. It can be frustrating to a new seller to think, "I have to do all of this to sell my stuff?" No, you don't. But, the more of it you can work into your listings routine, the more likely you will be to get sales.

Taking the time to create thorough, effective listings will save you time and headaches down the road. If you are going to be repeat-selling items (i.e., creating an identical item to sell over and over again using one set of photos), then writing one great listing can work for a long time if that item proves to be popular.

Think of your listings like setting up shop in a brick-and-mortar store. You don't just rent a building, throw stuff on a table, and expect it to sell. Store owners have to rent a space and renovate it to fit their needs. After that, they paint and decorate the shop to create the experience they want their customers to have. Once they're finished with the backdrop, they bring in fixtures and shelving to hold their goods. High-end shops are particular about fixtures because they enhance their displays. When they bring in their goods, they arrange them very carefully to draw their customers in and make them want to take a closer look at their products. Store owners generally carry through the quality and feel of their shop from the moment you walk into their store until they have completed the sale and bagged up your new purchases for you to take home.

If you have high-quality goods, then you want to showcase them in the very best light, with the right environment, displays, and layouts that draw your customers in and make them want to buy your goods. Even though Etsy is a virtual world, there is still a lot you can do to give shoppers a feel of quality and ambience that will entice them to stay in your shop—and the longer you can get customers to stay in your shop, the more likely that you will convert that business to a sale.

Creating a shop full of listings that appears curated and not just thrown together goes a long way toward attracting those customers who will stay and browse. If the ideal customer comes into your shop and it's her ideal shop, that's a match made in handmade heaven. It's up to you to set the stage so that when customers do find you, they will want to stay and browse. You want them to lose track of time, going farther and farther into your shop and looking at as many items as possible.

Now, I bet you're wondering just how to get them there. Well, there's a not-so-well-kept secret: SEO. SEO, or search engine optimization, is just a fancy name for Google juice. Google—and every other search engine out there, including Etsy—uses a set of algorithms it searches for when it is cataloging all of the websites in the world. When search engines scour the millions of sites on the web, they are indexing a series of markers that help them to determine which websites give the most relevant information to their users. All search engines are in business to give you the very best results that relate most closely to what you are searching for—so that you will return and use them again. Your job is to learn how to get the search engines to pick you as one of the relevant sources so your shop will show up when people search for what you are selling.

Did You Know?

Google is not only the largest search engine, but also the most visited website in the world.

Learning SEO

Hundreds of books have been written about the subject, but effective SEO boils down to two main things: finding the perfect keywords and using them repeatedly. Sounds simple, doesn't it? Well, it is, once you learn how. The better you become at narrowing down keywords and implementing them properly, the more likely you are to be found by customers using a search engine. Tapping into search engine traffic is the biggest way to grow any website, including an Etsy shop.

Luckily, you won't be wandering aimlessly in the dark, hoping to find the right keywords, because Google has a tool that will help you find the best ones. Google created its Adwords Keyword Planner Tool (https://adwords.google.com/keyword) to show advertisers looking to purchase ads with Google which keywords would work best to help customers find them. Website owners and managers across the web use it to optimize their keywords on any page now, so they can find the exact words and phrases that people are searching for most. Knowing the exact words that users are looking for is helpful because the more people that are looking for those words, the more likely you are to get in front of them.

Etsy Tip

If you are selling the same type of item for an extended period of time, occasionally go through the steps of checking your keywords to make sure that they are still the best, most relevant terms possible. Trends can sometimes affect the vernacular of searches.

There are a lot of boxes and buttons to look at in the keyword planner tool, but you really only need to know about a few of them for finding the best keywords for Etsy. First, you need to set up an account. It will take only a few minutes, and an account is free—so be sure to sign up (or sign in) to get the most out of the tool.

Then, you'll need to start with the barest, most basic word to describe your item. On paper, jot down every word you can think of to call a chalkboard tag, in every variation. Ask someone to tell you what he or she would call the item, too, because it might open up more possibilities you may not have thought about. On this list, you could call chalkboard tags:

- Chalkboard tag
- Chalk board tag
- Chalkboard tags
- Chalk board tags
- Blackboard tag
- Black board tag
- Blackboard tags
- Black board tags
- Chalkboard label
- Chalk board label
- Chalkboard labels
- Chalk board labels
- Blackboard label
- Black board label
- Blackboard labels
- Black board labels
- Chalkboard sticker
- Chalk board sticker
- Chalkboard stickers
- Chalk board stickers
- Blackboard sticker
- Black board sticker
- Blackboard stickers
- Black board stickers
- Organizing tag
- Organizing tags
- Organizing label
- Organizing labels
- Organizing sticker
- Organizing stickers

Looks repetitive, but those minor differences in wording and spacing can make a big difference in your search statistics. Once you have a list to start from, it's time to look up those words. Before you start typing in options, there are a few things you need to learn about using the tool for maximum benefit.

On the sidebar of the page, there will be several options. The main concern is to put a checkmark in the box that reads EXACT, leaving the others blank. Experts agree that this will yield the most accurate results, giving you a better indication of which words will work best for you in your searches.

After you have that box selected, it's time to move on to the main portion of the page so that you start to go through your list to determine the best options. Start by putting in the word that most widely describes your product. Sometimes, you may have two words that may be a good overall description. In this case, you could either look up chalkboard or stickers. With a quick search of both terms, you'll find that the word "stickers" has a search rate of 7,480,000 per month. The term "chalkboard" has a rate of 550,000 per month. Now, you may think that the obvious choice would be to go with "stickers" because the number is higher—but with the higher number of searches also comes more competition.

Competition is another key factor in choosing your keywords carefully. Ideally, you are searching for a keyword result that has a decent amount of search traffic, yet has a low competition rate.

- **High competition** means that there is a large percentage of websites that have the keyword in comparison to the amount of searches. If there are nearly 7.5 million searches per month and the competition is high, the likelihood of being seen as a small-scale shop is fairly slim. Unless you have an SEO genius on staff to provide you with top-notch work, you probably need to steer clear of those keywords.
- **Medium competition** means that there are several websites out there that have the keywords listed, but you may have a decent shot of getting seen if you maximize your SEO. I often choose keywords with a medium competition rate, because although there may be several websites out there that use those keywords, if you do it correctly you have a good chance of ranking fairly high. (I'm going to teach you how!)
- **Low competition** keywords are the holy grail of searches, but they are effective only if they have a large enough number of searches to warrant using them. If you can find a term with a low competition rate and returns of more than 200,000 searches a month, you have a winner.

As you go through all of your options one by one, write down the competition rate and find statistics for each one. You'll be able to narrow down your list to just a handful of good choices that way. You may find only one or two that are really strong, and if this is the case, then start adding other words that will describe the finer details of your item. If you create hats, then think of other keywords that can describe them: child, knitted, pink, character, etc.

You're going to need your main keywords, and you will also need to compile a list of thirteen additional keywords or phrases. We'll use these in the listing process to help your SEO.

As you list different variations of similar items, use some of the same keywords repeatedly, yet change the minor differences that make each listing unique. The more of a certain kind of item (say, hats) you list, the more search engines believe that you have the information that people are looking for.

When SEO-correct listings sell, those sold items will also help to solidify your authority on the subject to the search engines. If you have 100 listings for hats and have sold 150 listings for hats, you essentially have 250 pages that are all about hats. That's a lot of information that is all geared toward the same batch of keywords.

In the same light, if you sell a variety of items that all fall under one main umbrella, like home decor, then make sure that you are using the broader term as frequently as possible to draw in the traffic for the broad term. "Home decor" receives ten times the search traffic of "table runner." Adding those additional keywords will help make you visible to all of the searchers who are looking to find a more general term.

Keyword Comparison Chart

Use the Google Keyword Planner Tool to check your keyword options. Then compare the numbers and competition rates to find the best keywords.

Keyword	Search Results	Competition Rate
(e.g., stickers)	(e.g., 201,000)	(e.g., high)

Writing Effective Listings

Now that you have a big list of SEO happy words, let's put them to good use. The trick to making your listings maximize SEO is to use them over and over again. There are a lot of steps involved in writing a listing, but each one gives you an opportunity to increase your SEO. Each time you have a chance to fill in the blank with a word, refer to your word list and use those words, repeating them as many times as you can. Not all parts of a listing will use wording; some of the components are drop-down menu choices.

Who Made It?

You will choose from a drop-down box to select if you, one of your employees, or another person/company made it. If you handmade the item, you will choose the first option. If one of your employees made the item, then that would be the proper choice. If your item is a supply or vintage product, then you will choose the "another person or company" option.

What Is It?

In this drop-down list, you can choose between "a finished product" or "a supply or tool to make things." The finished product could be a handmade product or a vintage one, as long as the product is complete and ready for use. "A supply or tool to make things" pertains mostly to supplies. Some vintage pieces may also qualify, but if it can be listed as a supply, then you should mark it as such.

When Was It Made?

This timeline list includes all years (or decades) plus "not made yet." If your item was made recently (within the last two years), then it will still qualify for handmade. If you are marking it for vintage, remember that the item must be at least twenty years old. "Not made yet" items are products that are produced after the customer purchases them, also known as made to order.

Categories

Etsy uses a few of the options within the listing system for their own personal search engine purposes, and this is one of them. You can select from a huge array of choices, so just go through the list and find the one that best suits your item. You'll find two additional boxes that ask "what type," which are used to narrow down the item category to a more specific option. These do not affect your Google SEO, but they will make it easier for shoppers searching via Etsy to find your products if they are categorized properly. With millions of items listed on Etsy, shoppers find it useful to narrow down their search options using the categories to home in on the specific item they want.

Physical Item or Digital File?

Physical items are shipped via a mail carrier or hand-delivered. Digital files can be uploaded via Etsy and set to automatically download upon purchase.

Variations

Clothing sellers will find this part of the listing process useful, as they can sell multiple sizes or colors of clothing in one listing. You have the option of many different variation choices for your items, including sizes, colors, scents, and more. If your variation control isn't listed, you can even create your own. There are two sets of these, so if your color and size options vary, you can add the choices easily.

Photos

You can upload five photographs of your item—and you should utilize all five of these slots if possible. I will discuss photos in more detail later in this chapter.

Item Title

For maximum effect, listing titles should be at least forty characters long. Make your titles specific and to the point—this is valuable SEO real estate. Use the most effective words first, adding your other keyword terms to the list to fill in the rest of the title. Example: Chalkboard labels—reusable organizing stickers.

Description

Not only is this the portion of the listing that tells your customer what they are buying, it tells the search engine what you are selling. You should use the keywords at least three times within the body of the listing description. Using a keyword in the first sentence is crucial for building up SEO points. Repeating the same keywords in the listing at least three times leads search engines to believe that it is highly relevant to the search terms that you are aiming for.

Be sure to include any vital information about the product, including size, color, shape, style, etc. Also take this opportunity to explain why your item is special. Is there a story behind its creation? Will it make the customer's life better, easier, or more enjoyable? Tell your customers why they need your product.

Most of your shop visitors will land on one listing page for a specific product. Take the opportunity to lure them farther into your shop by including a link to your shop home page at the bottom of the listing description.

Even though you want to use lots of keywords to increase your SEO, be sure to also write as if you are talking to someone. Short, disjointed sentences are difficult to read and will only confuse your customers. This is your chance to have a conversation with them and make them fall in love with your item.

If you are selling supplies, make sure to include how you could use the product for a specific project. Most times supply sellers will have complementary items that will work well with the other supplies they are selling. If you have those types of supplies, you could also link to them within your description to help your shoppers find other products.

Remember that passion that compelled you to sell your products in the first place? Let that shine through along with your own individual personality. Shoppers will be drawn to items that are presented in the best possible light, so make it easy for your shoppers to be drawn in.

Shop Sections

You'll be setting up shop sections to divide up your shop, and there is a space in the listing system to choose exactly where your items will go (more on setting up sections later in this chapter).

Who Is It For?

Etsy has a system in place within the website to help shoppers find the perfect gift for their loved ones. You can specify whether a gift is meant for a man, woman, child, or pet, an option that can be especially helpful to some sellers.

Occasion

Just like the previous option, this is also for gift-shopping selections. If you have holiday-specific items, this is the perfect location to showcase them.

Styles

With nearly one hundred styles to choose from, you can pick the best descriptive style for your items. You have the option of choosing two styles, which can be helpful if your style doesn't fit neatly into one category. If you can't find the perfect description, you also have the option of creating your own.

Tags

Of all the places your SEO terms can go, this is one of the most important. You have thirteen Etsy tags, which is the equivalent of metatags on a traditional website. These act as markers to help repeat the keywords so that search engines can find your products. Use the most important keywords first, then work your way down to the least important. It is crucial to make sure that your search terms are captured in the tags section of your listing.

Materials

Some products are made with specialty goods that are highly desirable to customers, such as organic fabric. Use your materials section to showcase any unique qualities of your goods.

Price

Customers need to know how much your goods cost, which is why you have to set a price. Refer to chapter 5 if you need help pricing your items.

Quantity

Once upon a time, sellers paid per item even if those items were multiple quantities of the same listing. Now Etsy makes sellers responsible only for the first item; if that item sells, the product doesn't leave your shop inventory. Instead, it automatically renews the item and charges you for the newest item listed. It's a smart move to have multiple quantities available for items that can be sold more than once, because shoppers may need more than just one item.

Shipping

Although we will go into more detail about shipping later in this chapter, you need to include your shipping prices in the listing. Some sellers include the shipping costs in the listing and then offer "free shipping." It's not a bad option if your items are lightweight and cheap to ship. Shoppers are 90 percent more likely to purchase an item with "free shipping." In this section, you will also have the option to set up different shipping prices for different countries. When you create the first listing for this product, you'll want to weigh the package and use the website of the shipping company of your choice to figure out the shipping prices to several countries.

All of the elements involved in writing a listing are important, but the following parts are where you can take advantage of the SEO tools to make the most of your listings. Repeating keywords is the key to success!

- **Item title:** Use the most effective keyword.

- **Description:** Use keywords three to five times.

- **Variations:** Sizes and colors can be SEO triggers.

- **Tags:** List the most important first and the least important last.

- **Materials:** Eco-friendly options can boost SEO.

- **Photographs:** Name photo files using SEO-savvy keywords before uploading.

Using Analytics

Every shop on Etsy comes equipped with dashboard analytics to help you understand where your customers are coming from, what they are looking for, and which keywords bring them to your shop. Understanding all of this information is crucial to growth. In addition to the Etsy analytics, you also have the option of installing Google Analytics in your shop to understand in even greater depth how your shop works. When you have the combination of these two tools, you have a virtual overview of what your customers need.

Looking through either Google or Etsy analytics will enable you to see which keywords people use to find your shop. When you study the keywords, you'll notice that the most popular ones will most likely be the same with either analytics tool. Once you have those keywords, you know to make more of those items. When you add new products, focus on those that are working so that you can expand the listings to get even more traffic from your highest-ranking keywords.

If you have items and the keywords are not showing up in your analytics, you need to try new combinations for better optimization. Once you have done the best you can, then you will most likely need to work on your photography, because words can only do so much before photography must take the reins.

Perfecting Your Photography

In your digital shop, photographs are the primary means of drawing in your customers—especially from Etsy search engines. Potential buyers can decide in less than a second if they like what they see or if they want to keep on moving to the next shop. You have to learn how to compel clicks from searches into your shop.

Before you try to take immaculate photos that are national catalog caliber, let me share a secret with you: Drool-worthy photographs in catalogs such as Pottery Barn or Restoration Hardware are high-budget, six-figure productions that can require a whole crew of highly trained and crazy talented people to make happen. They can spend days and thousands of dollars to create the handful of images that are made public.

I didn't understand this in the beginning of my quest for immaculate photos; I only judged my abilities against those catalog campaigns. This concept became clear to me after having a long conversation with some photographer friends of mine, Diane Cu and Todd Porter (better known as the "White on Rice" couple). They're world-renowned photographers, shooting for such companies as Williams-Sonoma and Whole Foods. When I was down about how I'd like to capture more in my photographs, they told me to not be so hard on myself. They went on to explain that unless you plan on promoting your company through print campaigns (which alone can cost thousands of dollars), all Etsy sellers need are clean, clear photographs that accurately represent their items.

While it's true that all photographers get better with time and experience, and it's good to strive to have the most amazing photographs that you can, you also need to have perspective on just how far you can push your photography skills. In the very beginning, most shops just do not understand the importance of great photography. At the very least you need to have good, crisp images that showcase your products clearly.

Each photographer has his or her unique style to capture images, but your photographs will fall into one of two categories: images that capture your pieces in an environment or photographs that show only the product.

- **Environmental-inclusive photographs** capture your product in an ideal natural setting. These photographs will help customers visualize actually using the product themselves. For example, table runners displayed on a table will show what that piece would look like in a customer's home. Children's clothing is much more adorable on a child than hanging on a hanger, because it shows how the piece fits. Jewelry on a model is important to show scale.

- **Product-showcasing photography** allows your items to be the star of the show. You can capture texture, color, and size much better in a close-up photograph than you can in a modeled one.

Both types of photography are important for most products. If you can show your buyers how products will enhance their lives by capturing them in an environment, then you will be more likely to sell the product. However, having those showcase images will also let them look at it more closely and have a better view of the item's intricate details.

Once you understand the importance of great photography, you'd probably like to brush up on your skills to improve your images. It really doesn't matter if you have a top-of-the-line, fancy DSLR camera or a simple point-and-shoot—either way, there are a few things you can do to improve your images.

- **Natural, indirect light is your friend:** Never, never, never use a flash. Do not shoot at night or any other time of day that will not give you adequate lighting to take photographs without a flash. Natural daylight will give you the best results when it comes to color and clarity, but do not shoot in direct sunlight. Choose an indoor location near a window or a covered porch. Full-on sunlight will give too much glare, causing harsh and unflattering images. If you are trying to capture an outdoor scene where there is no shade, shoot your photographs on an overcast day.
- **Cheap foam core boards are your secret weapon:** From $1 to $3 each at most big-box or discount stores, foam core boards are a great supply to stock up on. You can use them in many different ways to improve your photos. If you are trying to get more light onto a product, use them to bounce the light from a window to where you need it for additional lighting. You can also use them as a backdrop for small products. Lay one on a tabletop and then use a box (or other large object) to prop up another board. This will create a "wall and floor" effect so that you have a completely white backdrop for your products. You can also use hardware-store clamps to act as legs to help hold up the "wall" portion. Want a black backdrop instead? Just spray-paint the foam core boards to get a completely different look.
- **Keep scenes simple:** Cramming too much pretty stuff into a photo will only confuse your buyer. You can use a few items to enhance the scene, but too much clutter can take away from the beauty of your products themselves.

You want the surroundings to make your items look better, not lost in a sea of things.

- **Use photo-editing software to enhance images:** You don't have to spend a fortune, but learning to use a photo-editing system will make your images clearer and improve less-than-perfect lighting. I highly suggest Photoshop Elements (for around $100) because it's easy to use and well worth the price. Some free options include Google's Picasa, www.PicMonkey.com, and www.Pixlr.com.

All skills in life take lots of practice, and photography is no exception. The more photos you take, the better they will get. Only with time will you learn the best locations in your house, which direction to aim the camera, and even what time of day works best. By the way, the time of day will change throughout the year, as sun cycles and daylight savings time will alter the pattern of sunlight from month to month. If you plan on taking photos regularly, make sure to schedule the best times of day into your routines so that you don't overlook prime photography time.

Want a good idea of what direction to take the style of your photographs? Think about where your ideal customer shops (besides with you). Your competitors have already spent hundreds of thousands of dollars on research to figure out what photographs their buyers want to see. Take your cues from those brands, but put your own unique spin on presenting your products in the best possible way.

Besides just taking good photographs and editing them to the best advantage, you also need to consider a few other things to optimize the potential of your images:

- **Name your photos before uploading with good SEO keywords:** No, this won't actually improve the image itself, but it will improve the likelihood of someone seeing it. Google search bots do not have the capability to look at the photo and determine what it is, so they go by what you name the photo. Customers looking to purchase a yellow scarf will not type in IMG_4568; they'll use the words "yellow scarf." If your photograph is named on your computer with those keywords before you upload, the image of your product will show up in search engine results and make your shop more SEO-savvy.
- **Watermark every photo:** Once you upload your photograph, you have little control over where it will go. I don't suggest a huge, overpowering watermark, but with the popularity of Pinterest, it's in your best interest to at least have a small one. You'll often find Etsy items listed on crafty or DIY Pinterest

boards. Putting your shop link directly onto the photo will help lead viewers back to the original source of the image.

- **Use all five of your image spaces:** Etsy gives you five spaces for adding photos of your product, and you should try to use every one of them. The more photos you have, the more at ease buyers will be about buying a product from an online source. Show close-up details and large overview shots. You can even add a photo of your item all wrapped up before shipping to show shoppers how much attention you pay to all the details.

Setting Up Sections

Thanks to Etsy, every shop has the option to sort their products using shop sections. If you have only a dozen items in your shop, then it doesn't really do a lot of good. However, if you have two hundred items in your shop, the section capability can help customers navigate your shop much more easily, making purchasing easier.

When customers land in a shop with hundreds of items, it can be daunting, especially because there are only twenty-four items highlighted on a page at a time. Shoppers rarely make it past page three, because typically online shoppers have a very short attention span. With the sections, you can determine when certain products in your collection fall into a narrower scope, making it easier for customers to narrow down your wares to see only what they are looking for.

Shop sections can be set up any way you'd like, as long as you have ten or fewer. Sellers can decide how they want to sort the items, but the smartest way is to take your SEO knowledge and apply it to your sections, giving search engines even more reasons to select your shop to be seen by search traffic.

I've seen a lot of shops set up fancy names for collections that are stylistically pretty and look artistic; however, as a business owner, you want to think about what is going to make the most impact financially. Understanding that the search engines can't comprehend that some fancy name is really a page full of links to home decor is powerful knowledge. Don't fall into the trap of trying to be cute or witty. Be basic, intentional, and smart when choosing your shop section names.

If your shop sells only crocheted hats, you could break down the sections by age or gender groups: baby boy hats, baby girl hats, toddler boy hats, toddler girl hats, teen boy hats, teen girl hats, adult men hats, adult women hats, and gender-neutral hats. Those specific sections will help the search engines understand that you sell hats, and lots of them. Shoppers will be happy because, if they are searching for baby girl hats, they can just click on the section link in your shop sidebar and see all the baby girl hats in one place.

Of course, for this to work properly, you have to choose the appropriate section in your listing process. Because it's not ironclad, you can freely move them around, rename the sections, or even delete sections and add new ones. Every aspect of each section can be changed, so it is a good idea to tweak it occasionally as your product line changes.

Seasonal sections are also a good way for shoppers to see which listings you have geared toward certain holidays. Put Christmas specials or other holiday sales on certain items together in one section so that your shoppers can take advantage of your specials all in one place. If your product line is somewhat varied, you might find other ways to streamline your shop through the use of listings:

- **Room by room:** Eclectic shops that sell home goods for the entire house can set up sections for each room (e.g., "kitchen" for towels or dishes, "bedroom" for pillows or blankets, "bathroom" for shower curtains or rugs, etc.). If items are clearly definable by which room they would go in a home, then sectioning by room might be useful.
- **Sizes:** Swimsuit or clothing sellers who cater to one specific demographic (like women) could set up their sections by sizes. Sizes are a specific measurement, so women might find sizing sections useful. Of course, if you are using the variations function inside the listing, then it won't work, because your item can go into only one section.
- **Styles:** Accessories sellers could sell more than one style of products to fit different preferences. Separating accessories into western, shabby chic, modern, etc., would give shoppers a clue as to what might fit into their closet the best. Most women don't stick strictly to one style, and it could be fun for them to click through the different styles to see what might work with their wardrobes.
- **Ages:** Producers of children's goods, whether they are clothes or toys, might make different pieces for different age levels. Directing items to sections meant for ages 1–2, 3–4, 5–6, and so on would give the shopper a clue where to start when shopping. This would be especially helpful for gift givers who might not know what would work best for certain age levels.
- **Prices:** Vintage sellers who have a huge variety of price ranges often have luck using their sections as a pricing guide. Items could be listed as: Under

$10, $10–$20, $20–$30, $30–$40, etc. Showcasing your ability to reach a customer on any financial level can be a great advantage to shops that don't rely on a certain style. Eclectic finds can be difficult to group together, so creating sections based on price range might be a good option.

Sections are meant to be dividers that help your shoppers home in on the items they need, without all the additional listings that might not pertain to them. Having clear, concise section names to define the different areas of your shop is another tool that will help your customers.

Think of it as a shopping mall: Your shop is the main building, but within that shop there are ten smaller sections to guide shoppers to the areas that interest them most. With just one click, they can narrow down all the items easily.

Etsy Tip

At the top of each section, each shop has an "All" section that includes every item in the shop.

Setting Up Policies

Working with people from all walks of life is invigorating, but it can also be frustrating if there are no policies in place to act as guidelines for your customers. If there are boundaries in place to protect both the buyer and seller, you will both have more peace of mind. Use specific and clear wording when establishing policies. There are several different spaces to set up different policies for the overall shop, including welcome, payment, shipping, returns and exchanges, along with a space for additional policies and FAQs (frequently asked questions).

Welcome

A short, friendly shop description is sufficient, but you can also use a few of those SEO keywords to describe your shop. This is also a good place to insert a tagline or mission statement, if you want to share it with your customers.

Payment

Collecting payment before shipping is a smart move for all shops. While customers have recourse for getting a refund from shops that do not ship items, sellers cannot do much about a payment if the item has already shipped unpaid. Therefore, adding in a policy about your available payment options is also important. Some sellers are comfortable taking checks or money orders via mail; however, the main payment method for sellers is either the Etsy checkout system or PayPal. No matter which method you prefer, be sure to lay out your policies clearly in the payment section.

Shipping

Explaining to your customers the ins and outs of your shipping process is crucial because every item you sell will most likely need to be mailed. There are some essential aspects of your shipping policy that you want to be sure to address:

- **How are your items packaged?** Are they sent in boxes, envelopes, or some special method? Do you use bubble wrap or shipping peanuts to package fragile items? Do you offer gift wrapping? Etsy sellers who use recycled packaging should make note of it here (and buyers generally love the eco-friendly recycled packaging).
- **Which shipping service do you use?** Customers need to know how to expect their packages. Including which method (priority, first class, standard, parcel post, registered mail, etc.) you use will also help them to understand your shipping practices.
- **What special services do you offer?** Online package tracking, insurance, or faster delivery may or may not be part of your original shipping fee. Do you charge extra for any of those services? If there are additional fees for those services, be sure to ask your customers to contact you for that information.
- **Which shipping address will you use?** Most buyers have their PayPal address and Etsy address set to be the same, but not all do. Let buyers know which address you plan to ship to up front so they aren't blindsided. If the address they provide is wrong, will you ship it again to a different (correct) address? If you are using the Etsy shipping system as your customer address book, make this clear in your policy so that customers will know where the package will arrive.

- **Shipping times:** This involves two factors: when it will leave you and how long the postal service should take. Once you've shipped several packages, you will gain a sense of how long it takes for a package to arrive from your area to other areas of the country or world. Letting customers know how long it will be before you ship the item and how long the shipping will take will give them a window of when to expect the package to arrive.
- **International orders:** This type of order may be held up for weeks at a time, so you should forewarn your customers. It rarely happens, but some countries can hold items in customs for up to six weeks. Telling your customer this up front will help them to avoid frustration over slow packages.

Returns and Exchanges

Every shop owner has a different opinion on returns and exchanges, and no single method is perfect for every shop. The nature of some handmade items might require specific sizes or personalization that will make it impossible to accept returns; other shops, like supply sellers, may have no problem reselling a returned item. While not offering returns might deter some customers from making a purchase, it's rare that it will turn away a seriously interested customer. Writing clear descriptions and taking great photos so your buyers will know exactly what they are getting will put them at ease if you choose not to accept returns. This is the most important policy, as the issue of returns will arise no matter how great your product may be. If you have outlined your policies clearly, you can refer to them when your customers ask about them. Here are a few other key things to cover:

- **Damages during shipping:** Will you cover this cost, or are you depending on the customer to purchase insurance if they think it is necessary? If you provide insurance on your packages, you need to note that customers must contact their post office for reimbursement.
- **If you accept returns, will you also refund the shipping price?** Clothing sellers might find that an exchange might be necessary, so will you charge additional shipping for the second item if a customer exchanges a product? Will you pay the return shipping for that customer to ship it back to you?
- **Do you need a reason for a return?** Accepting returns for any reason is fine, but if you have guidelines for reasons, then you should explain them in your policy.

- **What is your wait time for exchanges or returns?** Do you have a lifetime guarantee, or should customers contact you within thirty days? Do customers need to contact you within a certain number of days after receiving a package before they can file for a return?
- **Does the customer need to return the item in the original packaging?** If your items are packaged for retail or could be damaged beyond resale standards, then you will take a loss on that return. Create some standards for the quality of the return, just as you had for the quality of your product before shipping.
- **Will you accept returns on custom merchandise?** If you are providing customers with options for customization, you most likely will not be able to resell that item to another customer. If you cannot, then you'll be taking a loss on that product. You may want to have something in place for damages and so forth, but put specific guidelines in place for custom orders.

Additional Section and FAQs

Information that doesn't really fit anywhere else into your policies but needs to be addressed can go in the additional section. Policy writing is not the place to be fun and friendly (other than the welcome area). Use this space to let customers know things such as:

- **International customers are responsible for customs/duties fees:** This is especially important for shops that ship worldwide or are located outside of the United States.
- **Handmade items may vary slightly, but photographs are an accurate representation of the overall product:** If you are listing one-of-a-kind items, this won't apply, but sellers who take one photograph and then make replicas of the original to sell again and again will find that there are small differences between products. All large companies have this issue, too, so don't stress over the minor variations.
- **Computer monitor colors may vary, creating variations between the photograph colors and the actual colors:** The computer used to edit the photo can show a slightly different color from the one on the customer's computer. This is just a normal part of running an online shop, but you do need to mention it so that customers will be aware.

- **You should cover any small detail that a customer might need to know to understand your shop and make an informed decision under your policies:** If customers tend to ask the same questions over and over again before making a purchase, address them in your FAQ section.

Once you have written all your policies, be sure to use spell check and re-read them for grammatical errors. It is also a good idea to let someone else read them, just to be sure they are clear and concise without sounding rude.

Setting up professional, clear policies will help both you and your customer address any questions or issues that might arise. You can decide how strict or flexible you want to be with your policies, but having them there will give you a place to start.

Writing Shop Policies

Write effective policies using the categories below to help your customers feel confident purchasing from you.

- Welcome
- Payment
- Shipping
- Returns and exchanges
- Additional section and FAQs

Customer Service

Customer service can make or break an Etsy shop (or any kind of business, really). If you have seriously amazing customer service, the kind where your customers rave about their shopping experience on Facebook or Twitter, then you're going to reap the benefits of your actions long after the sale. Having horrible customer service (or no customer service) will have the opposite effect—and you don't want that to happen!

Great customer service is about having open communication, standing behind your policies and products, and keeping to the timeline that you have set. When doing all of these things, have a good attitude that will shine through in your actions and words, even if you decide to establish a formal business tone.

Keeping your customers updated on shipping times, sending production notes, and responding to their questions in a timely manner is crucial to building trust. If you are quick to respond, they will appreciate and remember your prompt service. When you answer them promptly, it shows that are you are attentive and dependable.

Even if you do everything perfectly, you will still face tough issues that will require grace and patience. No matter how good your customer service is, there will always be people who see things differently. Many times it is a misunderstanding on their part, but you should still handle them with the same level of courtesy as your happiest customer.

Turning an unhappy customer into a return customer is not easy. We're all human, and we all have those moments of being upset over a product or a service. Think of how you feel in that moment when you are at a restaurant and you have a horrible server who brings you the wrong meal and never refills your glass or checks on your table. Put yourself in the mind-set of that upset customer, and think about how you would like to be treated to turn the experience around.

It's a fine line—you don't want to hand out free merchandise and returns right and left, but you do want to make sure that your shop's reputation is of the highest caliber. Your shop is a reflection of you personally. You wouldn't be rude to a person face-to-face, so don't be rude on the Internet.

I'm not advising you to let your customers walk all over you, but I do think that you should politely hold your ground. If you are truly in the wrong, you should own up to it and do everything you can to make it better. If your product fell apart or wasn't delivered by the postal service, or even if you accidentally shipped the wrong item, then make amends on the customer's terms so you are both happy in the end.

Sometimes customers truly are at fault. They may not have read the listing correctly (because some do not read the listing description at all), or if they ordered the wrong item, it may not be your fault. Customers can overlook details you clearly spelled out in your description or policies or disregard the information entirely. Your job in having great customer service is learning how to handle these customers with as much grace as possible, so they are just as happy as the customer whose order was 100 percent perfect from start to finish.

Once in a while, customers who have a difficult transaction will leave negative feedback for you before you even learn about a problem they had. I'm not quite sure why some customers go straight to leaving negative feedback (they may have had similar issues with previous sellers), but if someone leaves you negative feedback, contact that person to try and resolve the issue. If you can settle the problem for that customer, you can send a Kiss and Make Up proposal (a feature on Etsy that gives customers a chance to change their feedback).

Maintaining a 100 percent positive feedback is not absolutely crucial, but if you can manage to keep it at that level it will be in your best interest. After you have several hundred customers that leave feedback, you will find that one or two negative feedback comments will not affect the 100 percent status. Because the feedback system only registers whole numbers, you have to fall below 99.5 percent for it to affect your overall feedback, which means you can handle one negative feedback comment per two hundred.

Personally, I have three negative feedback comments that I could not agree with the customer to reverse. It happens to even the very best sellers with thousands of comments and years of providing great customer service. A few customers even left neutral feedback comments, but upon contacting them I found that they weren't unhappy; they just saw neutral as a good feedback rating.

In the end, don't stress out about every single feedback listing that you get. On average, less than half of your customers will even leave feedback in the first place.

Of those that do, another half of them will only give a positive, neutral, or negative rating without a comment. Only about 25 percent of your customers will leave a feedback with a comment. Some sellers think that no feedback is an indication of a problem, but it's normal. Lots of buyers find your shop through Google or another search engine, then sign up with Etsy only to purchase your item, and they never go back to the site again. These one-and-done customers probably don't even know that they should leave feedback.

Besides dealing with direct customers, taking time to answer questions and reach out to those who talk to you via social media outlets is also a good way to publicly show your attention to customer service. If you show your attentiveness outside your shop, you have a chance to give people who haven't yet found your shop insight on how you do business. It gives you an opportunity to highlight your best qualities, draw those non-customers into the shop, and turn them into paying customers.

Grasping how important customer service is to your business early on will be a great asset. It's much easier to keep customers happy than it is to try to clean up messy situations with damage control. While it's not impossible to turn around the image of your business, if you can get off on the right foot and stay there, then you can build up a wonderful reputation from the time you open. Maintaining that friendly yet professional atmosphere can be your greatest asset, especially in a market like Etsy where the personal attention is a huge component of the entire site's success. Stay in tune with your original intent to provide the best customer service possible, and you'll reap the rewards for years to come.

Handling the Shipping

Selling tangible items online requires some form of delivery. Unless you are selling digital files of some sort, you will have to package and ship items. Getting those items from you to your customer will require additional time and expense. Chapter 4 detailed all the items that you might need to package your merchandise, including ideas on how to jazz up your packages before shipping. Shipping is a lot more complicated than just putting items in a box.

After you make a sale, you will have the information listed on your "Sold Orders" administrative page. This page details all items purchased by customers, whether or not they are repeat customers, where the items need to be shipped, as well as any special notes that customers may have left you regarding their order.

If customers paid via PayPal, you can also find their shipping address on your PayPal account page. Be aware that according to PayPal guidelines, you must ship it to the address listed on the PayPal receipt for you to be covered under their seller protection services. If you ship to an address other than the one listed on that receipt, then you may be forced to reship the package if it does not arrive or PayPal can remove the funds from your account. However, if you do ship to the same address listed in PayPal and your customer does not receive the package, PayPal will take your side if there is a dispute, providing you can prove you shipped the item with a receipt from a postal service.

Rarely does it happen, but if you have a package that does not arrive at the destination, some customers will bypass all communication and go directly to PayPal to complain. You will receive an e-mail from PayPal alerting you of the problem, which will need to be resolved within the PayPal website. Don't be afraid to call customer service if needed; they are very easy to work with. PayPal will work with you to resolve the issue so that both parties are satisfied.

When and how you ship your packages is completely up to you, but if you do not ship quickly after the sale, you need to let your customers know. If your items are made to order and you have a three-week lead time before orders will be produced and shipped, you need to be clear about the timeline.

When you get your orders ready to ship, think about your ideal customer. The first impression that customer has of your actual item is the packaging that it arrives in. If you can surprise the customer with some pretty yet simple packaging, it will make a great impression. Much like opening a gift, if the package and presentation are beautiful, you enjoy the unwrapping experience as a whole, not just the item inside the box.

Stellar Seller Tip

Making my packaging beautiful is important to me because I want my customers to feel loved and pampered. I use washi tape and stickers to close everything in crisply folded tissue. I even ordered stickers with my logo that say "Thanks!" with my signature, so every customer feels that personal touch. The last thing I do before I seal an order to ship is slip in a blank card or fold of tissue with that sticker on it, so it's the first thing my customers see when they open their package.

—Lisa Pennington, shop24.etsy.com

This is also the time to add a business card and even promotional cards if you have them. You have an opportunity to enhance your branding with a little extra attention to detail. It may seem like a waste of time, but once you have thought through your packaging plan, then it will be no harder than throwing the item in a box on the fly.

You took the time to carefully create the item, curate a collection of vintage goods, or select the perfect supplies, so show your attention to detail by enhancing your product with packaging that reflects your business's dedication to great personal service and the overall experience of your customers.

The packaging of your products might vary depending upon what you sell, but if you have an opportunity to include your logo or something that relates to your brand, take it. Jewelry sellers can package earrings on branded cards, party goods sellers can add a wrap or some trendy bits to enhance their products, or clothing sellers can add hang tags with care instructions.

Consider how high-end boutiques might package a similar item when you make a purchase in their shop, and give the same (if not more) attention to the details of your packaging. Customers of handmade goods love working with artistic people, so let your personality shine when packaging your items to give them one more reason to love your shop.

Going Global: Should You?

Etsy markets itself as the global destination for all things handmade. It has offices all over the world to stay in touch with perspectives from all walks of life. If you are a US seller and neglect to offer your goods to the rest of the world, you will be missing out on a huge segment of buyers. Tapping into the global market opens up far more opportunities than only selling inside your own country.

According to Alexa.com, 35 percent of all traffic on Etsy comes from outside the United States. If 35 out of 100 people looking at your items are excluded from the ability to purchase them, this will cut into your sales significantly. There are 20 million users on Etsy (as of April 2013). If you take out 35 percent of those users, you are eliminating 7 million customers from your shop from the start. It would be the equivalent to having a brick-and-mortar store where you tell every third person who walks in the door that you will not sell to him or her. An actual store would never turn away customers; you would lose too much business.

On the other hand, if you open up your shop to worldwide shipping, you allow your business as many customers as possible. We live in a global economy. People aren't as skeptical as they once were about buying from around the globe. If you welcome global customers into your shop, you'll find it much easier to reach the sales goals that you set for yourself.

Sometimes shops sell items that cannot be shipped outside their country. You must do the research to find any import laws that pertain to your products to determine whether or not they adhere to those guidelines.

Once you have determined that you can and will sell to a foreign customer, there are a few additional steps you must take when shipping your package. You will be required to fill out a customs form for all international packages. There is actually

International Shipping Restrictions

- **Food-related goods:** Most food items must go through the proper channels, which are highly expensive for an average Etsy seller. These include (but are not limited to) things such as fruits, vegetables, dairy, meat, seeds, and nuts. Candy makers will probably use a combination of some of those ingredients, so their products would be ineligible for international shipping, too.

- **Plant matter:** Plants and seeds are regulated due to pests and bacteria, which could cause problems if introduced to a foreign environment. Sellers who create planters with succulents (or other plants), as well as shops who sell seeds in any form, are restricted from shipping to most countries outside their own. Besides just seeds and actual plants, this includes wood, bark, moss, nests, grapevines, corn, straw, or any other natural material. Even some materials that you wouldn't consider being an issue might be scrutinized, such as herbal remedies or potpourri. If you are unsure, ask your local post office for clarity.

- **Animals and parts:** Selling products created using animal parts may be an issue. Starfish, seashells, animal teeth, porcupine quills, bird feathers, animal hides, horsehair, and wool are just a few of the animal pieces that cannot be used in a product that needs to ship internationally.

- **Chemicals and liquids:** Shipping liquid through the traditional post office isn't allowed, and shipping chemicals is also restricted. This may affect shipment of bath and beauty products to some countries.

more than one type of form through the US Postal Service, and your local postal worker can tell you which packages go with which forms. They are easy and self-explanatory to fill out.

Some customers might ask you to "mark package as gift," but unless the package actually is a gift to someone from them, you need to mark it properly. Filling out USPS forms is, in all honesty, filling out a government form. It is against federal laws to make false statements on a post office form, just as it would be to file your income taxes incorrectly.

Additionally, when you are dealing with international customers, you need to make sure you are clear with them in all communication that packages may take up to six weeks to arrive. You cannot control issues with customs or determine international shipping times. Most packages arrive in a timely manner, but sometimes shipments will be lost. The number from the customs form can help customers track down their packages through their local service, so if shipment seems to be incredibly slow, send customers that number to help them find their package.

Also be aware that international customers do not always use English as their first language. Sometimes communications with international customers can be difficult because they use translation websites to send their messages and to translate yours back to them. Do not use slang language, and try to be very precise with your words so things aren't lost in translation. Usually there is no problem with communication, but keeping in mind that this issue can arise will help curtail any language-barrier issues.

More Listings = More Sales

As any shopper knows, the bigger the store, the fuller the parking lot. Etsy is much the same: When you have a shop full of beautiful things, you get more sales. There are a few reasons why this is true, but the bottom line is that full shops (especially those that do all the right things) have more sales. And, because selling is the reason you run a shop in the first place, it might be good to understand the importance of multiple listings.

On the most basic level, imagine a high-end boutique that is beautifully designed, yet nearly every shelf is empty. There are a handful of things to choose from, which limits your ability to buy what you would like.

Now think about a big-box store like Target. Their high-end designs at reasonable prices draw you in, but you can never go into the place and walk out with only one thing. You find more and more that you put into your cart, which fills up fast as you are walking through all the aisles, admiring all the beautiful things. The designs are great, the prices are perfect, and the customer service is pretty amazing. You walk in to purchase laundry detergent, and two hours later you walk out with new clothes, something for your home, a few food items, other daily essentials, and maybe even the laundry detergent. And, bonus, you leave feeling great about all the amazing new things you just scored. It's a pleasant experience from entrance to exit in a calm, pleasing environment. You may even share a great bargain on your Facebook page or show off your new shoes on Instagram.

You were sucked into the whole experience—not just what you *had* to buy, but what you *could* buy—because a big-box store has such a huge variety of items. Successful sales is a numbers game, whether it is on Etsy or at the local supermarket. The more you have in your shop, the more likely you are to reach out to the person who is looking for the item you have. And once customers find you, they are much more likely to put additional items in their virtual cart if you have enough selection for them to be drawn in and spend more time.

When your ideal customer stumbles upon your shop, you want him or her to be smitten with your products, your photos, and your descriptions. Your goal is to get customers to click as many times as you possibly can so that they stay in your shop as long as possible. The more time customers spend in your shop, the more likely they are to purchase from you.

In addition to the shopping aspect, having more listings is important for getting the customers to find you through search engines to begin with. I like to compare SEO to filling a five-gallon bucket with sand: Each time you use a keyword, it adds a grain of sand to the bucket. It takes a lot of grains of sand to fill up that bucket, but if you keep adding them one by one, it will, over time, fill up that bucket. When the bucket is full to the top with keywords, your shop will come up at the top of searches.

Adding more and more listings gives you the opportunity to build up the keywords throughout your shop. Listing one hand-painted sign is great, but listing fifty of them builds your keyword levels up so that search engines will give you priority over websites that list only one sign. If there is another shop that sells fifty signs but is not SEO-friendly, then you will get more traffic.

Each time you sell one of your SEO-friendly listings, it adds even more grains of sand to the bucket. Every sold item has its own page, and all of those keywords count toward your overall SEO strength. It's the combination of the current listings plus the sold listings that creates your overall SEO score. (In chapter 7, we're going to learn how to use social media outlets to help your SEO, too.)

Choosing the right items to fill your shop isn't always easy. Be highly selective about the items you choose to represent your business. Every listing is an opportunity for you to reach out to potential customers and draw them into your shop. If your listings aren't up to par with what your customers are looking for, they will simply pass you by when skimming through the results. You can pull out all the SEO tricks in the book to get your items to the very top; however, if shoppers don't click on the items, all that work isn't doing your business any good.

Not only do the items have to be amazing, the photos must be great, too. Most customers do not read the words in the list of results; they look at the photographs. Your photographs have to pull them in and showcase your products in the best possible way. This is the magic combination: putting your items in the path of the customers so that they will grab them as they go by.

Be aware of the time of year if your items are seasonal. Not all products are seasonal, but shops that sell crocheted hats and blankets might not do so well during the warm-weather months of the Northern Hemisphere. This rings especially true if you are creating your products with wool, which means you may not be able to ship them internationally for the Southern Hemisphere to buy in the off-season, because you cannot ship animal products internationally. Try to develop some core products for your shop that could sell year-round. Crochet sellers might develop a line of handbags or headbands. No matter how you do it, you should have as much variety as you can fit into your shop, with a good mix of seasonal and non-seasonal items.

Conversely, if you ever find that you are getting too many sales (although it's an amazing problem to have), you can reduce the number of listings and it will slow down your shop a bit. Taking out a few items at a time will help you to keep within a reasonable production timeframe that will keep your customers happy.

Consistently adding new items to your shop creates positive energy. There is no way to prove it, but I have had many conversations with sellers over the years, and we all tend to agree: When you concentrate on your shop, putting effort and attention into it, you will begin to see activity. If you've listed five or six items, then waited for sales before moving forward, you probably won't see very good results. Tend to your shop regularly; do not let it sit idle. Working on new products, creating listings, quickly answering customer questions, and promoting your shop regularly are all ways to add momentum to your business.

Made to Order or Ready to Ship

Shops on Etsy function in one of three ways: items are made to order, products are ready to ship, or a combination of the two. No two shops function the same; it all depends on the wants and needs of the shop owner. Handmade sellers are typically the only ones with the luxury of choosing the route they want to take (hence the "made" to sell). Vintage sellers will need to find their stock before selling, and supply sellers may find that overselling can lead to problems if their wholesale source cannot fulfill orders quickly.

Ready-to-ship items are just that—ready to go in the mail at the moment of sale. All digital download available files are ready to ship, as they are premade and downloadable upon purchase. Vintage definitely counts, because you can't make something that must be twenty years old (unless your customers want to wait twenty years to get their orders). But handmade items are often ready to ship, too.

Shop owners who offer ready-to-ship handmade goods have a big stock of pre-made products. Lots of sellers find this route much less stressful. You get an order, you pack it up, and it's ready to go. Make more items, list them, sell, and repeat the process. As with all major decisions, there are some pros and cons:

- **Pro:** Shipping time is dramatically shorter (could be as quick as the same day), so your customers will receive their items more quickly, which always makes them happy. Happy customers are repeat customers!
- **Con:** Completely made inventory takes up space. If you are working in a small area, you may not have room to store inventory in addition to supplies and all the other needs of your shop.
- **Pro:** You can work at your own pace, building up inventory during the slow seasons. Listing each item as it is available will eliminate the stress of overselling.
- **Con:** Creating dozens of products can take a lot of materials, which means a bigger initial investment. Purchasing materials in many different colors or patterns to build up more varied stock can add up quickly.

Most shops that sell ready-to-ship items will make several of the items at once to increase productivity. Until you deeply understand, with a fair amount of confidence, what your customers will purchase from you, you may lose money buying materials that just do not sell as well as others.

When I decided to start selling pillow covers in different fabrics to bring a little more life to the aesthetics of my shop, I learned through a lot of trial and error that my customers loved aqua and turquoise fabrics in almost any pattern, yet rarely purchased reds. I figured this out by experimenting with a rainbow of colors, purchasing one yard at a time until I narrowed it down to a color family my customers preferred.

Variations in paint colors, fabric patterns, sizes, or shapes can all be tested, but you will have to use a lot of trial and error to determine what your customers will need, like, and purchase. Yes, it's true that there are customers for almost any product, but when you find the customers who return time after time, they will have a preference as to what they love about your shop. Pay attention to the sizes, shapes, and colors that sell the most, and build up your ready-to-ship stock accordingly.

Running a shop with ready-to-ship items is a great way to keep it running smoothly, stay on top of your orders, and keep your customers happy. If you intend to keep a regular full- or part-time job in addition to running a shop, this is definitely the way to go. Sellers who have the financial means to do so should try to maintain their inventory to keep their shop running in this fashion.

Handmade sellers who prefer to sell items made to order tend to deal more directly with their customers. If you find that most of the products you sell must be customized in some fashion, you will have to make the order after it is placed so that you can create the item according to the customer's specifications.

Altering sizes, colors, lettering, or any other aspect means you will be able to produce the item only once it has been purchased. Please do not create the item before you have been paid for it, because you never know what can happen.

Just like the shop that sells ready-to-ship items, there are pros and cons to the made-to-order shop, too.

- **Pro:** You can create a huge variety of products in your shop within a short amount of time with a limited amount of supplies, which is perfect for sellers who are starting shops on a shoestring budget.
- **Con:** A rush of orders might set back production times, creating a longer waiting period for your customers. If you are clear about your production time up front, most customers understand—but do not wait until they complain before addressing the issue.
- **Pro:** Less space is required to house only supplies, which might work better for those with a tiny work area.
- **Con:** Confusion between multiple custom listings can arise if you are not careful with your organization. Keeping clear notes is essential in getting the right package to the right person.

Running a shop to create every item after it is purchased can become very hectic during seasonal rushes. If you are predominantly made to order, try adding some ready-to-ship pieces. Some of your products might have very little variation and be basic enough to sell well year-round.

Stocking up on the basic items you want to keep ready to ship will help speed up your production time on the made-to-order items in your shop. Combining the two can help you make your shop the very best it can be. Learning to draw boundaries on which type of items to sell can come only with time and experience. Let your sales and customer requests mold your understanding of which direction your shop needs to go.

Considering Custom Orders

Etsy customers love having items made specifically for them. Shops can decide whether they want to take on all custom listings, just a few, or even none at all. Some categories are more geared toward custom orders than others, but all sellers should carefully consider if custom work suits their business.

Some shops may run for months or years and never take a single custom listing, but most shops will at least get a few requests to do special orders. Of course, if the main component of your shop is personalization (by embroidery, paint, size, etc.), then it might become the bulk of your work.

Before you decide to open up your shop to custom orders, you should ask yourself a few things. Do you like working one on one with customers? You may be e-mailing (or even calling) your customers for days or weeks if the project is complicated. You also need to have very good communication skills; you must be clear so that your ideas and the customer's ideas are one and the same. Misunderstandings can happen, but being as clear and precise as possible will help. Photographs of their inspiration and of your process will also help you to bridge the gap. If dealing with e-mails and daily communication isn't your favorite part of running a shop, then custom orders may not be the path for your business.

In addition to communication, you also need some organizational skills to keep track of different projects with various specifications. If you have only one or two orders at a time it might not be so overwhelming; however, if you have thirty orders, things can start to become mixed up very easily. Keeping track of the details of each project, along with the name of the customer it belongs to, can help coordinate custom orders more smoothly.

Sometimes custom orders do not require you to create a unique item; instead, you will create a mass amount of that item. If you make tapered candles and your customer wants two hundred of them for an event, the quantity difference between your set of two and the amount they need is considered a custom order. Can you handle the volume of the large order? Can you supply all the materials for it in a timely fashion? Will the production time be quick enough to meet the needs of the event? These are all questions you can ask yourself when deciding whether or not to take on a mass-quantity custom order.

Events like weddings can help a number of different types of sellers. The wedding market is a huge part of Etsy because brides love having special items for their big day. Wedding rings, dresses, shoes, bouquets, ring bearer pillows, ribbons,

Etsy Custom Order Policies

Etsy policy includes a section geared directly to the topic (all information available on their website). Below, in italics, are the custom order policies listed on Etsy's website.

- *"Custom order" listings must be listed for purchase with a set price.* If you are creating a listing for available custom work or requested custom work, you must include the price in your listing process.

- *The seller may use photographs of previous work and options for customization (for example: color choices) in the listing.* This is merely an option; you are not required to do so. Many shops have a graphic stating "Custom Listing" as a placeholder for the required one photo on the listing process.

- *If the seller offers different sizes or styles that affect the price, the seller must make a separate listing for each item.* If you are offering different options that can affect the price, each listing must be created individually. If you are offering a premium version and a standard version with different prices, then you need two listings.

- *The buyer must purchase the listing on Etsy to have an item created. Details about the customization can be discussed via Etsy Conversation or e-mail.*

- *If the buyer supplies their own materials to the seller for a custom order, they do so at their own risk.* Set a guideline in your policy for this situation. Will you take the risk of accepting someone else's supplies, such as a special fabric or paint that you cannot replace? (Personally, I've accepted these quite a few times and never once had an issue—but there are horror stories out there, too.)

- *The final custom item must comply with all of Etsy's policies for handmade items.* Whatever you sell to your customer, make sure that it follows all of the restrictions of the Etsy marketplace. Be honest, and remember that you reap what you sow.

- *When creating a custom order listing, be sure to select "Made to order" when prompted with the question "When did you make it?"* If you do not have the item in stock (and you won't for a custom order), then be sure to always choose "Made to order" when setting up a listing for that product.

- *The buyer must purchase the listing on Etsy to have an item created.* If you are contacted via Etsy for the purchase of an item, you are required to complete the transaction using the website. Although you are free to communicate with your customers via e-mail, you should not try to run the transaction "off the grid" to avoid fees. The fees associated with the order are the payment to Etsy for Etsy bringing you the customer. Also remember: The sold item will help your SEO if listed properly.

floral arrangements of every style, hairpieces, veils, programs, table linens, napkins, photography, photo booths, props, backgrounds, guest books, gifts for the wedding party, and invitations are only a few of the goods a bride can order on Etsy to put together her dream wedding.

If your shop is in the business of catering to any type of event, you will certainly get a lot of requests to have things made in special sizes, colors, and quantities to fit the needs of the customer. Sellers who cater to these requests can generate a steady flow of orders.

No matter if you are creating custom items for one person, one time, or for a wedding planner who loves your work and returns to your shop frequently, deciding whether or not you will take on custom work (and all that goes along with it) will help you handle the requests when they arise. You can go all out and take on every order you get, or you can politely decline—it's entirely up to you.

Custom orders are a huge part of my business, and I have only ever rejected three requests (due to limited time or resources). Personally, I enjoy custom work, because it allows me to do something different from the everyday studio work. Also, it allows me to deal one on one with my customers, which is my favorite part of the Etsy process.

Charging for Rush Orders

At some point in time, you'll log into your shop to find a request from someone who needs your item in his or her hands in only two or three days. While it's not impossible, it can definitely be an inconvenience to you. Wherever there is convenience in the world, it comes at a price. If you are saving your customers time by getting their items to them more quickly than the average transaction, they should pay for that premium service.

Customers who ask for special treatment are not only asking you to work faster, but also want to be bumped up to the front of the line ahead of all the rest of your customers. You will most likely have to work longer hours to get the order out on time (unless your item is ready to ship).

Additional pressure to produce items or ship them faster than originally agreed upon in the regular listing should come at a premium price. Some sellers may feel that rush fees are unreasonable, but I believe if a customer is asking you to work harder/ faster/longer than you normally would, then you should be compensated. In a job that pays an hourly wage, any overtime work is compensated with time-and-a-half pay. The employer is required by law to pay you an additional 50 percent of your hourly wage to keep you at work longer than forty hours a week. Therefore, if your customer is expecting you to work overtime, you should be paid for it.

The rush fee rate is different, depending on the type of work you do. Most shops charge an additional 10 percent to 50 percent of the product price as the rush fee. If you set this up front, then you shouldn't fret if people come to you and ask for this special service. Tell them your rate and explain why you charge it, if they ask.

Generally if a customer comes to you and asks you to ship a product overnight (which costs up to ten times more than standard shipping), he or she is probably not going to be worried about a small rush fee. Don't make it unreasonable, but do be sure to pay yourself for the additional work. Remember that convenience comes at a price, and your time is worth the additional fee.

07 Marketing Your Shop

You can have the most amazing products found anywhere online, finely made with attention and detail using the best quality supplies. You can package them with care and offer the most eloquent customer service. But if you don't have customers, then all that work won't equal money in the bank. You can take your shop to a great level with well-written listings that are SEO savvy and immaculate photos; however, to bring it to a full-time level, you will need to employ some marketing strategies to make the most of your shop's success.

Once upon a time, not so very long ago, marketing meant purchasing advertising either in print, on radio, or on television. Gone are the days of using only mainstream media marketing, and here to stay is the new world of getting engaged with your customers via social media. You can control the bulk of your marketing by doing it yourself—and who can sell your products better than you? I'm not suggesting that you should never purchase advertising, but why not start at the bottom of the budget and grow your shop via your own marketing efforts? It worked for Etsy, so if you are marketing yourself properly, it can work for you, too.

The best part of marketing: It fits into any budget. You don't have to have access to thousands of dollars to fit a marketing plan into your business—quite the opposite. The very best marketing for an Etsy shop is financially free, but it can take time to develop and maintain. You can certainly spend tens of thousands of dollars on high-impact print campaigns if you don't trust your own marketing skills; however, before you do that, let's take one more look at your brand.

The Importance of Being Branded

In chapter 2 we studied our ideal customer, thinking of every possible part of his or her life that would help you understand that person from the inside out. If you know your customers well, then you know where they are hanging out online. You want to be where your customers are; if they are hanging out on Facebook and you are hanging out on Twitter, you're missing a great opportunity. Before you start scouring the Internet to find your buying public, think about how you want to connect with them.

You want to woo your customer to come and shop with you, so, much like finding your life partner, you don't want to come up and spout off a pickup line that doesn't highlight your best assets. Thoroughly understanding your brand will help you choose the direction in which you want to take your marketing. If you want your shop to be seen as trendy and modern, then all your marketing visuals should reflect those choices. If you are going for a vintage vibe, take note of that, too. Your brand needs to be represented via any marketing materials in the light you've chosen to broadcast.

Consistently branding your shop throughout any marketing medium you choose is important. You need to deliver a clear message about how you want your business to be reflected. Thinking through all the choices is much easier if you learn to use your gut instinct as your guide. Remember, your unique style will shine through in everything you do, and it can become your signature. Knowing what works for your business and what doesn't is a huge hurdle to overcome, but if you can narrow all the millions of choices down to what you truly love and make it work, you can find the magic combination.

The combination of your logo, brand colors, photography style, writing style, and presentation will be one big recipe for your shop's overall marketing plan. Adding things into the mix without reason is definitely a recipe for disaster, so keep the overall scope of your business in mind when making choices so that you don't overload your customers. Keep it simple so they will be able to recognize your brand easily when they see it. The most recognizable businesses in the world use this same strategy, because simple really is the best overall plan. You can embellish your presentation from time to time, as seasonal sales might require, but for the bulk of the time keep your message and marketing simple and easy to understand.

When you finally do begin to find the core group of customers you are searching for, making them feel comfortable with—and excited about—your products is the main key. Customers who are comfortable enough with the quality of your goods and customer service will come back if you give them a reason. Structuring in excitement through promotions and new products is vital in gaining return business. Getting those customers to come back to your shop isn't nearly as hard as finding new customers from scratch.

Branding yourself will help prepare you to market your business with the absolute best results. Knowing what you want to promote, whom you want to reach, and how you want to draw them in will help you allocate your resources (whether time or money). Once you have made those decisions and are ready to start promoting your shop, you have to decide: Do you want to spend time or money?

Spending time on promoting yourself is part of the long hours in the day of a business owner. You can either choose to do the work yourself or to hire an assistant to do it for you (once you have enough business to cover the expense). As a handmade artisan, doing your own marketing is a way to connect with your customer beyond the scope of your shop, and building that relationship is vital to long-term success.

Not every single customer needs to become your new best friend, but recognizing customer names when you interact with them on social media outlets will help foster the bond between the customer and your shop. Because social media is the first place you should go when you are beginning to market yourself, you need to learn the outlets and determine the best one(s) for your brand.

Social Media Marketing

Before we get too far into talking about social media, I must warn you that it is an ever-changing world. Staying fluent in how each medium works is a constant battle, so instead of breaking down each option to the very last detail, I'm going to explain how they can be utilized to help you promote your shop. There are entire books written about each of the social media outlets, and they can walk you through the ins and outs of how they work. I'm going to explain *how* and *what* you should do to help you grow your business.

Don't get bogged down in expecting yourself to spend hours upon hours each day obsessing over how to keep up with every social media outlet under the sun, but instead try several of them out and see where you have the most success via clicks through to your shop or interaction with your customer base. For this portion, we'll call them your fan base—and you want to try to grow those fan bases on whichever outlets you use as promotion for your business. The more followers you have, the better.

Some of the social media outlets are accessed primarily through a basic website, while others are most often used through a smartphone app—but all of them are considered social media networks. There are way too many to discuss them all, so I'm going to touch on the most popular (and useful) in getting more exposure for your Etsy shop.

Whenever you are using any social media network, you have to first and foremost remember that it is labeled "social" for a reason: It is a place to interact with your customers. Social networks allow your customers to peek into your world, so be careful what you are broadcasting across these mediums. Remember to be courteous, professional, and kind. No matter what the situation, focus on the positive to show your business in the best light. Open networks like Facebook and Twitter are not the place to discuss a bad experience with a customer, because this just ends up making you look bad in the long run.

On the other hand, social networks are the place to praise your customers, share their rave reviews about your products, and show them how much you love being a part of their lives. Everyone likes to be appreciated, and publicly showing your appreciation will only help to deepen the relationship you have with your customers.

Did You Know?

Three of the top ten websites in the world are social media networks: Facebook (number 2), YouTube (number 3), and Twitter (number 8).

Facebook

If you are going to utilize only one form of social media, numbers alone make it evident that it should be Facebook. It's the second most popular website in the world, just behind Google. You already got your SEO in order in chapter 6, so the next thing on your agenda should be to start building a following on the social media mother ship. Facebook has more active users than any other website, so your ideal customer is without a doubt using it.

Before you set off in search of a magic formula to score thousands of fans overnight, let me put your mind at ease: Slower is better. You don't have to have hundreds of thousands of fans on Facebook for it to have a positive impact on your shop. Even as few as one hundred followers who truly love your shop and want to stay updated on your new listings or sales can be a great resource for your marketing.

Finding those fans is fairly easy on Etsy because you can link your Facebook page to your shop. The "like" button for your page will show up in your shop announcement on your shop home page, so new customers who stumble upon your shop can become new fans without ever leaving your shop.

Another easy way to build your following is to provide a link to your Facebook page in the thank-you note you send to customers at the end of their transaction. Entice customers to actually follow through on that link by telling them you offer exclusive discounts and specials to Facebook fans. Of course, you have to follow through with those specials, but it's a great incentive to share a coupon code every now and then to keep your customers coming back for more.

In addition to sharing links online, include your Facebook URL on your thank-you or business cards, in your shop newsletter, or in any other communication lines you use in your business. Of course, if you have the opportunity to share only one link, you want to make sure it is to your shop. Once you have the customer in your shop, there is time to offer the Facebook link upon completion of a sale. Translating your customers into fans is the main goal for continually marketing to them long term.

There are ever-changing rules and regulations on Facebook, but the main keys are to use the header space for your brand. Because you can use only a small portion of it as wording, it will better serve your shop to use a good photograph of one of your products, or a collage of several of them, to help people who find your Facebook page before they find your shop page.

Let's take a quick look at some of the features you can use on Facebook:

- **Tagging people and pages:** If you are friends with a person or like a page, you can link to their Facebook page when writing your own posts. Not only will it help people discover other people and pages, it also alerts people that you have mentioned them on your page.
- **Sharing other people's/pages' posts:** Underneath each post there is an option to share the post on your personal or fan page. This is a great tool to use when you find someone who shared your product on their page with a fan comment or project.

- **Researching analytics:** Studying the amount of traffic, shares, likes, and comments your posts receive along with the times and days you have posted them is beneficial because you can pick up on follower trends, including when they see your content most. Using this information to put together a schedule of what and when you will post to Facebook will make your time much more manageable.

- **Scheduling posts ahead of time:** Take advantage of this great feature to set your posts for the week and forget them. Don't think you have a schedule to devote hours a day to being on Facebook; scheduling means you don't have to! Choose one afternoon a week, then sit down and plot out what posts you'd like to put up for the following week. Setting up your posts in advance lets Facebook do all the work for you while you are doing other things. Do make sure to check in occasionally to interact with your fans, because posting without ever answering replies won't help build the sense of community you should be striving for.

- **Private messaging:** If you use Facebook as a home for flash sales (discussed later), buyers can comment on your post for the item. After the customer has agreed to purchase the item, you can use Facebook's private message system to solidify payment and shipping details so that their information isn't visible to everyone else.

- **Adding on apps:** Right under the header portion of your page, there is the ability to add on applications (or apps for short) to promote other social media channels or your shop. With the click of a button, without ever leaving Facebook, your followers can browse your shop and make purchases. The less customers have to work to find your shop, the better chance you have of making a sale.

No matter how great your page looks, unless you are sharing good content through Facebook posts, your fans will not be active. Offering a diverse stream of posts will help you to engage your fans, making them want to participate in your posts. Need ideas on how to engage them? You can use:

- **Questions:** People love to give their opinions on almost any issue, so use this to your advantage. Asking a funny question pertaining to your business can help those who normally remain silent to chime in. Supply sellers might use prompts such as "What's your biggest craft fail?" so followers can share their funny stories. Asking your customers relevant questions about your business can help you gauge their opinions without seeming stuffy. Jewelry makers could even use simple choices like, "Gold or silver?" Seasonal questions are good for any type of shop, because the goal isn't just to get followers to purchase; you simply want them engaging in conversations.

■ **Customer features:** Offering your customers a discount on future orders in exchange for them sharing their recent purchases on Facebook is a great way to entice them to help spread the word about your shop and your Facebook page. Use the sharing option to highlight the customer's post on your page as a sign of thanks for his or her amazing support. This will make that customer happier, and it will also show potential buyers who follow you how much you appreciate them. Some shop owners not only share the posts of others, but quote comments or feedback they receive via Etsy as testimonials. When you are sharing these glowing reviews, be sure to show your sincere appreciation and love to your customers; no one likes to see constant bragging.

■ **Photos and ideas:** Great photography is the eye candy of Facebook. If you make pet items, showing adorable puppy photos is the perfect way to keep drawing in your fans. Make home goods? Beautiful rooms and spaces that complement your style are sure to please the customers who pamper their homes instead of pets. Posting photos is a great way to catch new eyes, but when you are sharing, please do so responsibly. Don't steal graphics or images from sites without giving proper credit (which might be as easy as tagging someone). Photos of listings are great, too, especially if you have new items you want to showcase.

■ **Daily stories:** Happy and uplifting stories are a fun way for fans to see behind the scenes of your world. Handmade sellers tend to make a stronger connection with their customers, so fans appreciate hearing about a funny line from your child, a crazy antic of your dog, or any other small glimpse into your life that showcases what makes you unique.

■ **Flash sales:** Even though this is independent of Etsy, offering items for sale on Facebook can help bring customers over to your shop. Before your sale, use a graphic to promote the "Facebook Only Flash Sale," which will consist of a limited number of products at reduced prices. Choose five to ten items and post a photo of each to Facebook, all within a few hours of one another. Give fans the details about the product and the price (plus shipping) within the text of the post. Be sure to be present for the entire sale so you can answer questions about any products. Most sellers who utilize this method give the sale to the first person who comments, "Sold." After the sale is complete, message or e-mail the person for his or her PayPal information and shipping information. It's a simple way to clearance out goods or to quickly promote new listings. Those who see the item after it's sold will be able to purchase one at regular price in your Etsy shop. Remember all that great service you put into your shop to entice repeat customers? Use the same loyalty for Facebook customers and it will have the same effect.

- **Coupon codes:** Offering a quick-turnaround coupon code is a great way to reward your Facebook fans for following your page. Gifting a free item with a $50 purchase (or whatever amount you choose) is only one way to spread a little Facebook fan love. You could also make an exclusive coupon code and share it only on Facebook. I don't suggest making this a regular habit, but to occasionally offer 10 to 25 percent off orders can provide a great boost if you find yourself in a sales slump. Personally, I only offer coupons about six times a year. I've found that it is in my best interest to offer them sporadically, rather than putting my sales on a schedule. If customers know when sales will be, they may delay purchases waiting for those codes. When offered as a surprise, then you might pull a sale out of someone who otherwise wouldn't think to purchase at that time. This combination seemed to work best for my shop; however, as with all small businesses, you have to experiment to find what works best for your unique situation.

In addition to working on your own Facebook page, private groups are a secret gem. Private groups allow you to connect with other Etsy sellers to help cross-promote, share wholesale sources, offer advice, or just find friends who will understand your life better than your non-Etsy friends. It's easy to find groups by doing a quick search, or reach out to Etsy friends to see if any of them can invite you into a group. Still can't find one? Invite a few sellers with whom you've built friendships to come together to create your own support group.

Day	6 a.m.	Noon	6 p.m.	10 p.m.
Monday	Product of the day photo	Question to encourage interaction	Funny story or anecdote	Tip or tidbit of relevant information
Tuesday	Coupon code	Product of the day photo	Question to encourage interaction	Customer appreciation shout-out
Wednesday	Question to encourage interaction	Funny story or anecdote	Tip or tidbit of relevant information	Product of the day photo
Thursday	Show studio behind the scenes	Customer appreciation shout-out	Product of the day photo	Question to encourage interaction
Friday	Tip or tidbit of relevant information	Question to encourage interaction	Share photo of product in progress	Product of the day photo
Saturday	Product of the day photo	Funny story or anecdote	Show studio behind the scenes	Customer appreciation shout-out
Sunday	Flash-sale item photos	Product of the day photo	Question to encourage interaction	Tip or tidbit of relevant information

Paid Advertising on Facebook

Facebook tends to make things harder and harder on companies trying to promote their goods on the mega-site. On average, less than 25 percent of your followers will see any given post. This is intentional on Facebook's part, as its business is to loop you into their advertising plan. Companies can pay a fee to have their posts promoted to a larger audience, much larger than the page can reach by itself. Starting at $5, you can get your post onto the feed of additional users; however, this doesn't necessarily mean that those users will become your followers. Some pages have seen great success with this option; others seem to gain no additional benefit.

If you are looking to promote a large sale (like a Black Friday event), then it is worth the risk of trying to push the sale out past your own audience. Just remember, though, that those who see the ad will not all be your ideal customer, so the chances of getting the sale from those Facebook users are not as great as from the ones on your own particular page. Using post-promotion advertising can be a new way to bring in new fans, if they like what they see.

Want advertising that bypasses your page and goes directly to your shop? Facebook has that option, too. Just like almost every other website in the world, the sidebar of Facebook has a row of ads, and you can purchase space that links directly to your Etsy shop. The best use of this purchase-only space is to pick your very best item and use it as the photo, along with a great catch line to entice people to click through to see your shop. You can set your own budget, and Facebook will show the ads until you run out of money, at a price determined by how many thousand times the ads are viewed.

Overall, if you have only ten minutes a day to devote to any social media, then you should use them on Facebook. I completely understand that you never seem to have enough hours in the day to run an independent business (aka "indie biz," for the cool kids), but maintaining a Facebook page should be one of your top ten priorities to keep your shop running.

YouTube

As the second-largest search engine, YouTube has a following so large that your ideal customer is definitely using it. After all, the Google-owned video website is known for its massive audience, which watches four billion videos on YouTube per day. Let that sink in a minute.

With four billion videos watched every day, you can only imagine what finding a fan base on YouTube could do for your Etsy shop. Even a small following can have a huge impact on your shop. It's a highly underutilized social media outlet for Etsy sellers (though there is no shortage of videos on the site to help you grow your own shop). Highly integrated with all things Google (including Google+), YouTube links to your shop can help increase your SEO, among other benefits:

- **Promote your own commercial—for free!** Of course, if you want it to be seen (or better yet, go viral!), then you need to make an amazing commercial.

Don't think people watch them anymore? Go look up the commercials on YouTube from last year's Super Bowl; some of them have six million views! Let's face it: It's highly unlikely you will get millions of views, but even a few hundred might bring some people to your shop. The best commercials are funny ones—short, to the point, and amazingly written. You don't even have to have a fancy editing system; just a simple video program can help put yours together.

- **Use it as a video catalog:** Photographers can benefit from a video-style portfolio of their very best work, set to music (copyright-free, of course) that suits your photography style. Jewelry makers can also follow suit, showing models wearing some of their best-selling or newest pieces. Think of it as an automated lookbook to show off your shop.

- **Show how to do something:** Sharing ideas on how to use your products or make something with them is an ideal way to maximize your exposure on YouTube. People typically go online to be educated or entertained, and if you can do both at the same time, you might find a great following. Supply sellers can share craft projects on how to use their products to create something fun. Sell hair bows? Try doing videos on how to do hairstyles to showcase your handmade goods. Any way you can integrate your product into an informative video can be helpful not only to your audience, but to your shop as a whole.

- **Talk about your shop philosophy:** Getting personal with your story will allow followers to see inside your mind, your creative process, why you do what you do, and, above all, the heart behind your business.

Sharing via YouTube can be a smart move, especially if you've got time to produce great content. You can also cross-market the videos on other social media channels like Facebook, so your following on other networks can find your videos for even more reach.

Unlike some networks where you should try to be highly interactive with your followers, YouTube requires much less energy. Simply post your video, promote it where you can, and occasionally answer questions. Actual interaction on YouTube isn't as high as on other social media areas, so the demand on your time isn't nearly as high as on Facebook or Twitter.

If you are the focus of the video, let your personality shine through. If you're quirky, go with it! If you're more low-key, that's great, too. Be yourself, because you have more of a chance with video to let people see you for who you truly are. Handmade sellers who find a huge following generally do so because of their personality. People want to connect with them, to see a real human instead of a global corporation.

Tips for Taping

If you've decided to dip into the YouTube pool but have no idea where to start, don't worry. Here are some tips to get you started:

- **Start with your laptop video cam:** There's no point in buying a super-expensive high-definition video camera only to find out that you hate videos and never want to do a second one. Using your laptop camera is perfectly fine, but if you find yourself getting tons of views, you might want to upgrade eventually.
- **Set your own stage:** Creating video tutorials means that you are putting the information front and center, so you want your video to have a fairly neutral background. Setting up your space in front of a blank background might be too bland, so look for an area that's neat and represents your brand. Also be aware of lighting issues when picking the place to make your videos.
- **Light it up!** Just like with photographs, you want to pay attention to the lighting of your video shoot. You definitely don't want it to be too light or too dark, but also look at the style of lighting. Natural daylight works best (just like for photographs), so try to schedule taping around the best daylight.
- **Tape in batches:** Doing multiple videos in one day will make much better use of your time. If you are the focus of the video, you will need to do your hair, makeup, etc., only once. Just change your outfit in between to appear different for multiple videos. Depending on how long your videos will be, you can easily do four or five in one afternoon. If you're releasing one every couple of weeks, you can create a month's worth of content in a single day.

Adding some videos to your social media marketing is a great plan, even if you don't focus directly on the products themselves. This adds another layer to your social media marketing platform, creating more depth and connection between you and your customers. The more you connect with them, on any level, the stronger your business will become.

Twitter

Spelling out your message in 140 characters might not always be easy, but it is the short burst social media outlet with a long list of followers, including major celebrities, everyday moms, and even the president of the United States. Signing up for Twitter is quick and easy, and it can help you reach out to your customer in real time.

Etsy makes it easy to connect your shop and Twitter account with a follow button located on your shop's home page (right beside the Facebook follow button). In addition to the main page itself, Etsy also provides a button to make it easy for shoppers to tweet out products they love, with a Twitter button located on each individual item page. With one click, shoppers can share their finds with their followers, complete with a shortened link leading directly to your item.

Twitter is a fast-paced medium, probably the fastest of them all. Of course, to make the most of it, there are a few tricks:

- **Hashtags happen:** Just in case you don't know, hashtags start with a # sign, immediately followed by a phrase all stuck together with no spaces (example: #HashtagsAreHotOnTwitter). They are clickable and will take you to a page full of recent tweets sharing the same hashtag. Some people use them for identifying tweets (#Etsy is a hot hashtag), but others use them to point out irony or to be funny #EvenIfTheyAreNotFunny. You cannot use spaces, characters, periods, or commas, as they will break the hashtag. Hashtag abuse isn't recommended, but some Twitter users are self-proclaimed addicts who can't help themselves (and I'm one of them!). Etsy sellers often use these hashtags to help find each other: #Etsy, #Handmade, #IndieBiz. There are several Etsy promoters on Twitter who re-tweet Etsy-related posts, which can help new followers find you.

- **Re-tweeting is sweet:** Re-sharing things you love from other Twitteraholics helps to build up a sense that it isn't all about you and your shop; you want to be part of the larger community. It's an easy way to add some content to your Twitter stream without being the original creator. Moderation is the key, so re-tweet only the best of what you find. You want to be seen as a source and not a spammer.

- **Talk to the customer:** Twitter followers can be turned into customers if you show them the right thing at the right time. Don't just talk at them, talk with them. When you ask questions, people will answer. Reply so they know you are listening. For me, the easiest way to keep up with replies is via iPhone, because it's so easy to keep up with what's happening through notifications. Make sure that you use their handle in your reply (like @shabbycreek—that's me!). When you use their Twitter name in your tweet, they'll get an alert to know someone has mentioned them.

Apply the same theory to finding a Twitter following as you do for a Facebook page: slow, true, friendly fans. The more active you are, the faster fans will find you, but it's not always easy when you're trying to juggle a shop along with five or six forms of social media. Still, you want to feel as though you're tapping into every possible market.

Before you begin spreading yourself too thin, don't stress out: You can schedule tweets. To make the most out of your social media schedule, you can sign up for free social media management application sites such as Hoot Suite (www.hootsuite.com) to put both Facebook and Twitter together on one dashboard. Hoot Suite also allows you to preschedule your posts on both Facebook and Twitter, which you can do without toggling back and forth between the two.

Besides just allowing you to set your Twitter schedule ahead of time, Hoot Suite has a built-in link-shortening tool. When you have only 140 characters, shortening a 60-character link down to a 12-character link gives you more space to be descriptive. Otherwise, you'll be taking up most of your tweet with the long title of your Etsy listing that shows up in your product URL. If you're tweeting real time, you can use a link-shortening tool, such as Bit.ly (https://bit.ly), which will not only make the links shorter, but also track them for you so you can tell which links got the most traffic. When you are building your following and still learning what works best for your business, this is a wealth of information. Pay close attention to those numbers so you can learn which day(s) work best for promotions and utilize them in your schedule. While Hoot Suite does offer the option to choose the schedule for your posts based on the peak times from your following, learning what to tweet when will be crucial in making the most of your Twitter feed.

Twitter Tip

Don't always use all 140 characters of your allowance on Twitter. Leave room so that if people want to reply, they have space to add a little something extra to your tweet if they quote you.

Want to have even more fun with Twitter? Integrate your Twitter and Insta-gram accounts so you can share photos. Letting followers see behind the scenes into your day, whether it's the process of creating something new, giving custom-ers a thank-you shout-out with a preview of their package, or even just what you do after the workday is done, allows another level of opening up your world to your followers. It's also a fun way to get more interaction with customers on yet another social media network.

Instagram

In the beginning, only iPhone users could enjoy the world of Instagram. Now one of the fastest-growing social media platforms is available on both Android and iPhone systems, but you still have to have a smartphone to use the photo-sharing app. Instagram is a quick snapshot into the world of its users, who range from teenage band-fans to grandmothers to even pets who have their own dedicated pages.

Monthly users total more than 100 million, with an average of 40 million photos a day being shared. If you're a smartphone-using small business owner, you should be on Instagram. The unique thing about Instagram is the involve-ment of its users; the average follower to interaction ratio is much, much higher than any other form of social media. Where a Facebook page with 14,000 fans might average a dozen or so likes per post, an Instagram user with only 1,000 followers might average 50 likes per photograph posted. Even if fans don't own a smartphone, they can interact on the Instagram website to like or comment on photos.

With all the other social media forms available, why is this one so beloved by its followers? The Instagram community is amazingly supportive. Members share photos, engage in conversations, and let their guard down a little more than they would on other networks, because it's primarily capturing the spur of the moment, which humanizes people.

I know you're probably tired of reading about making a "connection to your customer," but it truly is the one thing that will set you apart from all the other shops. There are very few superstars in the Etsy game who aren't connecting with their buyers on multiple levels. If you want a fun way to visually connect with your fans, Instagram is your answer.

You can still have a presence on Twitter and Facebook, even if you do not regularly write posts specific to them. Adding your Facebook and Twitter accounts to your Instagram profile will allow you to cross-promote your photographs across all three social media forms, yet only do the work of posting photos to one site. Hashtags will translate on both Facebook and Twitter; however, user names don't always have the same fate. If users are consistently using the same name on Twitter and Instagram, then the use of tagging names will work. Facebook, however, uses a different algorithm, so the tagging will not work between the two sites.

Understanding Instagram is easy enough, but new users might wonder, "What in the world can I do with it?" Well, you could:

■ **Share new products, in their ideal environment:** Because Etsy allows you only five photographs, sometimes you run out of ways to portray products with nearly unlimited uses. Supply sellers can take quick photos of items that can be made using their products. If you use your products personally, then occasionally share where you use them yourself. Add your shop address to the end of the post, so when sharing it on other platforms it will become a live link. (Sorry, the only live link on Instagram is in your profile—so make sure to utilize it.) By simply adding www.YOURSHOPHERE.etsy.com, the link will become live and easy to click for those on other social media forms.

■ **Ask for opinions on colors, shapes, or sizes:** Can't decide which new color to add to your product options? Snap pictures of some paint chips and ask followers to tell you their favorite. Letting customers share their voice is a great way to make sure you are in sync with their wants, sometimes helping you improve products in ways you might not have thought of on your own.

- **Have an Insta-sale:** Much like the Facebook Flash Sale, having an Instagram-only sale is a great way to make use of a following. Just make sure that you don't duplicate the content on Facebook, or you'll have to keep up with two social media streams at once to finalize orders. Avoid confusion by creating your own unique hashtag to keep the stream of photographs together in one place.
- **Share an Instagram-exclusive coupon code:** Use a graphic app like A Beautiful Mess to create a simple graphic with your shop address and the coupon discount plus code to reward your Instagram followers. If you plan on running the sale on other networks, be sure to drop that live link in!

Building up your following on Instagram isn't much different from other networks—you just have to get out and join the community. If you only ever post your own photos but never follow others and become interactive, you will never grow. To be interactive you have two options: liking photos or leaving comments.

Liking a photo on Instagram is similar to giving a thumbs-up to a post on Facebook. Simple and quick, you can either click the heart button below the post or double-tap the image to give it a little love. It's a quick way to show support to feeds from people you follow. Being among the first ten people to like a photograph will give you another perk: Your name and Instagram link will show up below the photo. When the photograph gets more than ten likes, it rolls over to a number, but by clicking on the number, you can see a list of the people who liked the post.

Commenting isn't any different from on any other social media, but it seems to be a bit more popular on Instagram than on other platforms. Taking just a few seconds to type out a comment will not only show support, it will also show your name as the writer of the comment, so you will gain even more visibility.

Commenting and liking photographs is a good way to find new followers, but please be authentic. If you're only leaving one word (e.g., "nice"), then you'd be better off stopping at a like. If you engage with those you follow, your followers will become engaged in what you are doing. Shallow comments will only get you shallow followers, and those are not your ideal customers. Be real, be you, be genuine.

One more layer you can add to your Instagramming is to use hashtags. Funny ones can get more reaction from your current followers, but basic hashtags might help you find more new followers. Some highly popular hashtags, like #DogsOfInstagram, are full of people who love to share photos of their furry friends. If you're posting lots of pictures of your pets, find hashtags that will let the animal lovers find you more easily.

Both funny and basic hashtags are great to use, but you need to use the right kind with the right type of post. If you're posting a photo of your products, using basic tags will be much better for your post. Just posting a funny photo of your latest craft fail? Then a funny hashtag is probably a better bet.

Selling on a digital platform, such as Etsy, you'll be able to understand why photographs are so important. Your photos are a digital representation of your products. The more photographs you have of your products, the better chance you have of reaching someone who will fall in love with them.

Pinterest

Rarely does a website come along and change the face of social media, but Pinterest has become a game-changer for almost every website. Traffic to the pinboard-style photograph collection website grows monthly for almost any company who utilizes the free service. Etsy sellers are no different from any other website owner; your main goal is to bring in traffic.

So what makes Pinterest better than other forms of social media when it comes to marketing? On average, according to Rich Relevance (www.richrelevance.com), Pinterest shoppers are spending significantly more per order than any other form of social media, averaging $140 to $180 per checkout, versus an average of $80 on Facebook or $60 on Twitter. Of course, Rich Relevance is the firm that studies marketing for massive retailers such as Amazon and Walmart, but it's interesting nonetheless. If you look across the board, Pinterest users have an average household income of $100,000 per year, Facebook users average $69,000 per year, and Twitter users average $45,000 per year. The higher up the income scale, the more money people have to spend on wants versus needs. And, just to be clear, the average yearly income of an Etsy user is $25,000—a huge difference!

If your goal is to find the highest income bracket within social media, Pinterest users are the group you want to target. To make the most of the powerhouse traffic generator, you'll be pleased to know that Etsy makes it easy with a "Pin It" button located right on the sidebar of every listing. When customers find something they love but aren't quite ready to purchase, they may pin your item to one of their pinboards. And that's the beauty of Pinterest: Much of the traffic is user-generated, so you don't have to do much work.

So how can you make use of the website? Pin your own items. Don't just sit back and wait for passive traffic. Be proactive. As with any social media platform, the more followers you have the better, but there are ways to get your items seen:

- **Using keywords:** Although Pinterest wasn't built with the primary objective of becoming a better image search engine than Google Images, often users will turn to Pinterest when looking for products. Searching for a chevron table runner on Pinterest will give much better results than a Google Image search. If people are pinning from your item page, your title will be automatically filled into the text box. Remembering the SEO words will be handy here, too, because people use the same basic words on Pinterest that they do on Google.
- **Joining group boards:** Group boards are when one person starts up a pinboard on Pinterest, then invites other pinners to share their links on the board. These are essential to find, because often the board will have a much

larger following than your own personal boards, which may be newer. To find one, do a search for boards using keywords like "Etsy sellers," and search for boards that invite users to join by leaving comments on pins or have an e-mail address in the board description. Sellers who don't have a huge following of their own can take advantage of the traffic of mega-boards by choosing ones not only with the largest number of followers, but by looking at the number of repins. Repins by their followers will show engagement, which is the ultimate point of Pinterest.

■ **Offering "pin it to win it" contests:** Major brands, including retailers like Pottery Barn, have found great success in offering giveaways for people who use Pinterest to help promote their products. Although you'll need to use your other social media channels to promote the contest, offering fans a chance to win a shop credit or even a particular item is a fun way for them to interact with your shop. If you're going to offer a giveaway, make it a good one—the prize has to make it worth their while to take time out of their busy day to promote your business. A $10 candle won't be much incentive; however, a complete set of ten different candles could be seen as a good deal. You can ask them to repin a certain graphic that leads to your shop's main page, or ask them to pin any item from your shop. Thinking outside the box to make it a fun contest followers will want to enter (and win) is the key to making this type of promotion work well.

All forms of social media work best if someone is paying attention to what you're doing, but to get followers you can't just pin your own products. Curating a collection of pins to represent your Pinterest presence can help you show off other aspects of your business. If you make items related to kids, having boards that reflect other parts of the lives of moms who buy from you is smarter than only pinning your own items. Adding in birthday party ideas, easy kids' crafts, and simple lunch recipes will make your ideal customers want to follow you. Occasionally sharing your items with an audience will help them be better received, in a more natural (and non-spammy) way.

Followers sometimes stumble upon a pin through a search, which leads to a certain board, which may lead them to your main Pinterest page. When they land on that page, your main goal is to make them want to follow you. Having a clean, precise page will be the easiest way for you to showcase your brand. Once you get your account in order, you'll find it easier to maintain your page in the future. When you're getting your virtual Pinterest house in order, consider these tips:

- **Put boards representing your brand at the top:** You have the option to move boards around on your board page, so organize them to your advantage. Boards representing the ideals behind your brand should be at the top; then work your way down the list. Group boards should be on the very bottom of your page (unless you are the owner of the group board). Don't make your products the highlight; instead, information from other sources to solidify your brand's identity should be front and center. Supply sellers might have different boards to represent different products, such as glass crafts, wood crafts, etc. Home decor sellers should be pinning home tips, decor trends, cleaning advice, anything to show your followers how to pamper their homes beyond just buying from your shop.

- **Create a board for your shop:** Having a home for your own items is a good way for you to gather all the pins for your items in one place. It's also a great way to have a virtual showcase on Pinterest. As you pin your products, be sure to include the price in the description (this will automatically pop up when you add a dollar sign), because pins with prices receive much more activity than those without them.

- **Pin from the original source—always:** There is no bigger Pinterest sin than clicking on someone's pin and finding the wrong website, a bad link, or no information whatsoever. The major reason for this is lazy repinning, where you like the idea but don't take time to ensure it leads to the correct information. If you see something you'd like to repin from someone else, simply click through to be sure the pin is going to the correct place. If all your pins are clean and safe, your followers will trust you, which is always a good thing for any type of business.

- **Use good, solid descriptions:** Pinterest is gaining a reputation as a good search engine, so make those searches easy by using SEO-rich keywords. Commenting with quick words like "LOVE!" to explain a beautiful table runner won't land you in any search results; you'll end up buried by the thousands of people who aren't working to maximize pins. Do your best to briefly describe the information behind the pin, not just the photograph itself.

- **Fill out your profile:** Pinterest allows you to link up Facebook, Twitter, and even a personal website so that you can interconnect with other platforms. Use your description to give a short synopsis of your brand. Your logo can go in the profile image, but you can also use your own photo if you are trying to be seen as a handmade artist. Because you get to choose your Pinterest name, choose your brand name if at all possible (just another thing to check on if you choose to start a new brand).

- **Like, comment, and repin others:** Repins are fairly normal, but comments aren't as frequent as with other forms of social media. They're actually sort of rare. If people you follow pin something you like, let them know with a quick comment. Your profile will pop up in their feeds as the commenter, so their followers will see your brand, too. Once again, don't spam every pin you see just to be seen, but leaving honest comments can lead more people to click through to your boards and follow you.
- **Pin at the perfect times:** Because Pinterest is such a huge force in driving traffic to websites, large companies have paid research firms obscene amounts of money to learn when to pin. You want to pin when people are on the site, because the more traffic there is on Pinterest when you pin, the more likely you are to be noticed. Any time Monday through Friday, 8:00 p.m. to 1:00 a.m. Eastern time (US) is the best time during the week to schedule your pins, but almost any time on the weekend is a good time to be active on Pinterest.

Pinterest doesn't have its own built-in scheduling system to preset your pins, but there is a solution that can help. ViralTag (www.viraltag.com) is a subscription-based website to help you make the most of your marketing schedule, and you can preset your pin schedule. Because pinning regularly is the best way to steadily grow your audience, taking advantage of ViralTag might be the best use of a small marketing budget. For a small fee, you have access to set up your pins when you have time, rather than being on the computer at hours that might not mesh with your schedule.

If you are pinning great content, on a regular schedule, onto uncluttered boards, behind a solid profile, you'll find a following on Pinterest. It's not difficult to learn the ropes of the site because it's built on a simple platform that engages people. If you don't oversaturate followers with your promotions, you might find that Pinterest is a good way to share your shop with an ever-growing base that loves to share with others.

Google+

Google+ may not be the trendiest social media site, but the benefits of using it are so great that you shouldn't ignore it. Because Google is, well, Google, you know if they are pouring money into creating a social media community, then you should participate for the SEO benefits alone. Sharing your shop on Google+ is a great way to build up links that will increase your shop's SEO value.

Google+ has some great features that are quite different from other platforms. Whereas some social media sites allow self-promotion but discourage an overabundance of it, Google+ was built to give you multiple ways to promote to your heart's content, such as:

- **Placing live links in your profile:** When you are putting together your profile page, you have room for the links to each section of your shop to showcase your products. You also have room at the bottom of the sidebar on your profile to add all your other social media platforms, such as Facebook, Pinterest, Twitter, and YouTube.

- **Using Hangouts on Air feeds to YouTube:** Hangouts on Air (HOA for short) is a way for you to record video in real time. Not only will the video be live on your Google+ page, after it's finished it will automatically be transferred to YouTube with no additional steps. HOAs are a fun way for subscribers to see an unedited version of you, one that cannot be faked or chopped up in any way. You can also invite up to seven people to be on the video with you, so it's a great way to hold a roundtable-style discussion on a topic.

- **Building SEO with +1s and shares :** If your friends or followers on Google+ like what you post, they can either give it a +1, share it, or comment on it. When others +1 your posts, it gives your content a little more authority in the eyes of Google. If people share your post on their streams, then others can see your original post, which means even more eyes will see what you've got to say. Of course, just as I've said for every other form, +1ing and sharing other people's posts are great ways to build up some Google+ relationships.

- **Hitting on hot hashtags:** On your stream page (that's the main page you land on when you sign into Google+), down on the side you will see a list of trending hashtags. If you click on the link, you will see a long list of other hashtags that are the most used at the time. If you can provide content that suits the hashtag, add a post and engage in the trend so that new people can find you. If it's near Mother's Day and you've got the perfect gift, let people know about it by sharing a photo of the product, your link, plus a short description of the item with the #MothersDay hashtag.

- **Joining communities:** Within Google+ is a huge network of communities for every interest you can imagine—including Etsy sellers who are looking to join forces with other sellers for their own support group. Use these groups as a network to share and learn experiences, gain more knowledge, and even cross-promote each other.

Google+ users are the most Internet-savvy of all social media users. They're brands, bloggers, and the Internet elite who are on the pulse of what's hot. Although it may not be a mainstream social media outlet like Facebook, people with much better SEO than you can find you through the lesser-used platform. Connecting with them is much easier because they want to be seen and heard on the network. Reach out to them and listen to what they have to say, and generally they will listen to you in return.

One Last Note about Social Media

Taking advantage of social media marketing is the best thing you can do for your business. Not only do your posts build an awareness of your products, the everyday interaction about your daily life will develop a relationship with followers. This is the step a lot of busy shop owners want to avoid until they're in sales slumps that almost put them under. Being consistently active on social media will keep your brand fresh in the minds of those who love your style, want your products, and will support you long term as a small business owner.

You don't have to use Instagram or Twitter as an ongoing diary of your life, because no one wants to know what you're up to twenty-four hours a day. But staying in touch with your audience is the key to keeping conversation fresh, relevant, and interactive. Don't just talk *to* them; talk *with* them. Conversely, get to know them a little better, use them as your jumping-off point. Social media is the best way to stay in touch with your ideal customers so you know what they need in life and how you can provide it. If you listen to your customers, they will reward you with incredible business growth. Be real, be true, be your own amazing self. Your brand is built upon your own style, so keep faithful to what makes you unique.

I know there are a lot of ways you can get bogged down in social media, but the truth is you only need to find two or three sites that fit your life and your business mission. If you hate Twitter, then don't tweet! Learn to make social media work for you, because a little bit of effort in pre-scheduling can have a huge impact on the success of your Etsy shop.

	Sunday	Monday	Tuesday	Wednesday	Thursday	Friday	Saturday
Google +	2 posts	2 posts	2 posts	2 posts	2 posts	2 posts	2 posts
Pinterest	5 pins	5 pins	5 pins	5 pins	5 pins	5 pins	5 pins
Facebook	4 posts	4 posts	4 posts	4 posts	4 posts	4 posts	4 posts
Instagram	3 posts	3 posts	3 posts	3 posts	3 posts	3 posts	3 posts
YouTube	1 video	None	None	None	None	None	None
Twitter	5 posts	5 posts	5 posts	5 posts	5 posts	5 posts	5 posts
Blog Post	None	1 post	None	1 post	None	1 post	None
E-mail	None	None	None	None	None	1 e-mail	None

What about Blogs?

Before we start learning all about blogs, I'm going to admit something up front: I may be a tiny bit biased. I've been a blogger for longer than I've been an Etsy shop owner, so blogging is near and dear to my heart. As a blogger who has worked with Etsy sellers for several years, I know how to maximize the success of working with other bloggers, as well as how to utilize a blog to market your Etsy shop. Blogging is one of the most effective ways to reach any audience, whether you prefer to work with other bloggers or take on the task of writing your own blog.

Starting your own blog is the cheapest way to promote via blogging, yet it can be very time-consuming. Unless you aspire to be the next big blogger, you really need to update your blog only a couple of times a week—so don't feel pressured by the daily posts on some mainstream blogs. A blog can be mostly personal or all about business, but if you are only ever talking to customers who already know about you, then it can be a waste of time. Instead of constantly blogging about updates, try to vary your content to reach out to a larger audience.

Although you can certainly pay huge amounts of money to designers and create a customized, highly expensive website, starting a simple blog on a free platform such as Blogger (www.blogger.com) might be a better option in the beginning for a few reasons:

- **It adds no cost to your marketing:** Well, it can add time, but financially it's smarter to choose a free platform, and if you decide you want more control over your website design, you can upgrade later.
- **Custom platforms can take longer to learn:** Using Blogger is very easy and quick to learn, so you can go from absolutely no blog to having one up and running in just a few minutes. If you don't have time to devote to learning a new skill, the process can seem overwhelming. WordPress.com (www.wordpress.com) is also free, but it takes a little more effort to learn.
- **There's no pressure of payment:** If you're paying to host your own blog, like with WordPress.org (www.wordpress.org), you might feel pressured to make the most of your money.

On the other hand, you may decide you want to pay to have a custom blog designed because WordPress.org offers many plug-ins and add-ons that are not available on Blogger. No matter which platform you use, Etsy offers a widget you can put into your sidebar called the "Etsy Mini" to help promote your shop by showing photos and providing live links to those listings.

Etsy sellers may find that blogging becomes a way to connect with readers who become customers. In the first few months of my own blog, I shared tutorials on how to make your own home decor, and several of my readers encouraged me to offer my goods for sale because they didn't have the tools or skills to make them themselves. After receiving tons of e-mails and encouragement from my readers, I opened up a shop to offer some products for sale.

Imagine my surprise when, six months after opening my shop and only a year after starting my blog, I was starting to make more money than I was from my day job. I was blown away by the support I received from readers who became customers, and customers who became readers. I built my business by monetizing my blog and selling my products on Etsy, so building both the blog and the shop was important to me. If I slacked on blogging, then my shop definitely suffered from the lack of traffic. Every month my blog was the number one traffic source of my Etsy shop.

Other bloggers who put effort into writing a good blog also see their blogs as the number one traffic sources for their shops, so I'm definitely not alone. The key is putting forth the effort. Building a blog following is relatively easy, using the same social media tactics we discussed earlier in this chapter—especially those involving

Pinterest. Pinterest and blogging go hand in hand, but the key is providing content that people want to bookmark and remember.

Readers frequent blogs for one of two reasons: to be educated or to be entertained. The best bloggers combine the two, showing how to do something while entertaining readers at the same time. If you're a handmade seller, you can quite easily work your products into your blog posts, simply by showing different ways you use them. Not every post needs to highlight your products, but much like Pinterest, you want to put together a well-rounded content package to help your readers learn something to enhance their lives.

Supply sellers can definitely take advantage of blogging, because it gives them a platform to show customers step by step how to use the products they offer. Easy-to-follow tutorials are the most shared blog content on Pinterest, which is a major traffic source for most tutorial-based blogs. Instead of excessively linking to your shop a dozen times within one post, simply tell readers where they can purchase your supplies, either in a supply list or through a link at the bottom of the post.

On my own blog, I shared tutorials on making your own home more beautiful on a budget, often featuring the very products I made to sell. If you have a skill that might deter someone from doing the project themselves (like sewing), there will be readers who want the product yet will not make it, so they will just purchase it instead. Sure, there will be people who would rather make their own, but, honestly, those people are not your ideal customer. Most people who are crafty or skilled enough to make their own pillows can simply look at a photograph and make it themselves, even without instructions. Look past the people who want to make your items, because you aren't trying to sell to them.

Long after I published the original French script curtain tutorial on my blog, it would occasionally show up in random posts that had nothing to do with the curtains. The original photograph I used as my listing photo was taken in my own kitchen, because the very first set I made was for my own personal use. After the post was featured all over DIY blog land, people began asking me to add them to my shop. Whenever I shared a photo of my kitchen, even without mentioning the curtains themselves in the blog post, I would get a frenzy of orders for sets upon sets of curtains. It took a couple of posts for me to grasp what was happening, but I began to add items from my shop to my photos once in a while, and it would always result in sales of whatever item I used, without one link to my shop other than in my sidebar.

The moral of the story is, don't push your products on your readers; just use them naturally. Soft sells are much better for your readers, not only because constant promotions will deter readers, but because authentic content is so much more believable.

On top of all of the entertaining and educating, be a little personal. Blogs who find a strong following also let readers see the person behind the screen. Share stories about your dogs, your kids, or a horrible weekend. Not every single post needs to be a set of instructions; you need to humanize your writing so you let your personality shine in the post. Handmade sellers especially need to make readers feel like they're having a conversation with a friend, once again, building trust between you and your customers. When readers become more invested in your story, they are much more likely to purchase from your shop, because it is like buying from a friend versus a random big-box store.

Readers who become customers will give you shout-outs on their own personal social media sites, be more likely to share your shop with their own friends, and become your own cheering section. This is a powerful resource for a small business. But if you really want to make the most of blogging, forming friendships with other bloggers can be some of the best networking you can do to help your shop.

Working with other bloggers through advertising can be a great way to get your brand in front of an already established audience. When a seller connects with a blogger whose audience is full of their ideal customers, it can be like hitting a gold mine of traffic to your shop. Finding the blogger who is your perfect match isn't always easy, so take the time to get to know the blog before contacting the blogger about advertising for your shop.

The easiest way to be seen on blogs is to simply purchase a sidebar ad. Some blogs offer small ads linking to your shop for as little as $10 per month. Larger blogs can charge upwards of $1,000 per month for the same size ad, but blog ads are like most things in life: You get what you pay for. If you're ready to invest a little money in advertising and want to start with blogs, consider a few things before you buy:

- **How many page views does the blog receive?** Most blogs charge for ads according to the amount of traffic they receive, but the numbers can be a little deceptive. Look around on the blog to see if you can find a link to a press kit or advertising page, which usually includes monthly traffic statistics.
- **Do readers interact with the blogger?** Page view numbers are a good jumping-off point, but you also want to look at a blog's interaction rate.

Most blogs offer readers the option to leave comments, so look to see if they are receiving any. Comments are a good indicator that readers slow down long enough to actually see the ads on the sidebar, as it takes much longer to write out a response than to simply read and leave the blog.

■ **Are readers sharing posts on Pinterest?** You can see the pins of any blog by going to its source page on Pinterest: http://pinterest.com/YOURWEBSITEHERE.com. (Sorry, doesn't work for Etsy shops!) Look at the blogger's recent posts and compare it to the source page. Is the most recent post getting pinned? If so, the blogger probably has a more interactive audience.

■ **Does the blogger's content and style match your brand?** If your shop is all about farmhouse-style vintage goods, yet the blog is geared toward hip, trendy teens, you are probably looking at the wrong blog. You want to find someone whose audience will appreciate your goods, not scoff at them. There's a blog for everything you could ever imagine, so keep looking.

Locating the perfect blog does take some time, but finding it will be worth the effort. Before you start to invest money, take a little while to get to know the bloggers. Read their posts for at least a few weeks so you can grasp what kind of message they convey. You're looking to find a blogger whose business ethics align with yours, someone who cares about his or her readers the same way you care about your customers.

Once you find the blogger you'd like to work with, try a sidebar ad for at least a couple of months, so you can gauge how much traffic it sends you. At the end of your ad run, look to see if your traffic from the blog was worth the price you paid for advertising. Before you start doing math equations to map out your success, you really need to wrap your head around how advertising works.

Advertisements don't automatically equal sales. The point of an advertisement is to create awareness of your brand. You don't watch a soda commercial on television, automatically stop what you are doing, drive to the store, and buy the soda. The point of the ad is so that next time you are at the store to purchase a beverage, the advertised brand will stick out in your mind and be familiar to you. You'll instantly know the brand because of the advertisement. Brand recognition is huge, even for small businesses, because the next time customers need to purchase a product you make, your shop will be in their mind when they begin to search.

Testimonials and reviews work quite differently from traditional advertisements. Bloggers who have built a following might be able to share your products with their readers, either through a post or via a social media shout-out, and you may get a far better response than you would from a sidebar ad. Because a blog post is similar to the front page of a newspaper, the cost of this type of ad is usually much higher than a sidebar, but this kind of advertising can be ten times more effective.

Blog posts that contain substance, not just a testimonial, are far more likely to have residual traffic for months and years to come. Supply sellers who partner with bloggers to create projects and share tutorials based on their products can see huge traffic, especially if the blogger promotes his or her post through social media channels. Large craft companies run campaigns with bloggers quite frequently because, in most cases, it works much better than traditional media advertisements.

While there is a plethora of bloggers out there with smaller blogs who are more than happy to do product reviews for absolutely free, be cautious of handing out your valuable products to the wrong blogger. Carefully choose the bloggers you would like to work with, and rotate from time to time if you want more exposure. No blogger is prominent enough to be the sole advertising support of a shop, so try to grow your marketing through connections to at least a few blogs, possibly in different niches, so you are making the most of your marketing.

Working with bloggers isn't the only way to spend your advertising dollars, but because blog readers are Internet-savvy, they are more likely to include your ideal customer than any print media outlets.

Sample Blog Post Schedule

Sunday	Monday	Tuesday	Wednesday	Thursday	Friday	Saturday
	Shop sale promotion		Story behind product		Tutorial	
	Life as an artist		Lifestyle post		Behind the scenes in the studio	
	Product promotion		Customer appreciation and love		Tutorial	
	Story behind product		Funny story		Feature another Etsy artist	

Traditional Media Advertising

Traditional media advertising is not used quite as often as online advertising; however, you might find it to be the perfect element to round out your marketing plan. In nearly every magazine you open these days, you can find an ad directing you to an Etsy shop. Depending upon the readership of the magazine, traditional ads can sometimes be a better buy than ads on larger online websites.

Almost every magazine, newspaper, radio station, and television channel offers advertising rates, usually found on their websites. Some offer website advertising in addition to their main outlet, which might be a good fit for your shop as well.

Newspapers and magazines aren't the only option for print advertising; business cards, postcards, brochures, and handouts are all considered part of print advertising. You can share them with perspective customers who might have an interest in your shop. Jewelry sellers who participate in home jewelry shows might even offer catalogs for their customers to browse. Any printed material used to promote your business can be considered an advertisement.

Landing Print Features

Have you ever dreamed of seeing your products on the pages of your favorite magazine? You can make those dreams a reality! It may seem scary at first, but reaching out to share your products with the editors of major magazines is the best way to land your product on feature pages.

Editors scour Etsy every single day to find items they can use in photo shoots for editorial content. They want to feature beautiful handmade items. They are looking to add some fresh, new products for their readers, and Etsy is the perfect place to find them. While you may be lucky enough for editors to come to you (hey, don't laugh—it happened to me), you can also take control of the situation. Don't just wait for features to happen—go after them. We all know that fortune favors the bold, so take a risk!

Reaching out to magazine editors is fairly easy; you just have to know how to find them:

- **Start by purchasing the publication** (or at least reading it thoroughly at your local library): You need to pitch to publications your ideal customer will be reading. If your product is the wrong fit for the readers, you'll be doing work for nothing. But if you are a good fit, you want to be able to effectively communicate to the editor of the magazine why you are a great fit.

- **Identify the editor:** Before you put that magazine away, look at it one more time to find the name of the editor. Just behind the table of contents for a magazine and the note from the editor, you will typically find the magazine's masthead. Listed on the masthead is every editor who works for the magazine, usually listed by subject. Find the appropriate editor and take note of his or her name so you can do a little more research.

- **Google the editor:** Do a search for the editor's name, along with the magazine title, as in "Joe Smith, *Bride Monthly*." Searches generally lead you to people's LinkedIn (a professional networking site) pages, which can help you to find them on other social media platforms. If you can, find them on Twitter or Instagram to learn a little more about them so you can be a little more memorable when you e-mail them.

- **Take note of their editorial calendars:** Magazines generally work four to six months ahead of the season, often doing major holiday work up to one year ahead of time. If you are going to pitch a seasonal product, make sure you are sending queries at the appropriate time. Turnaround time is often very tight for editors, so if you do offer to send them something, make sure you can get it out very quickly.

- **Decide what you want to offer:** Although product features are great, you might get more traffic if you offer editorial content to magazines. Do you sew? Submitting sewing projects for full tutorials in their magazines will get you more page space than a small photo of a product. Personally, I've had my home featured in decor magazines, products featured in major bridal publications, and DIY projects featured in craft magazines. I found a better response to the project and home photos than I did for plain product photos. No matter what type of content you are offering, be sure you can meet those quick turnarounds.

- **Learn their guidelines:** Every magazine has submission guidelines, usually posted on their website. Familiarize yourself with these rules, because breaking them will only make you look unprofessional—plus it's a waste of time to do things wrong. Get off on the right foot with the editor and you'll have a better chance of making a great first impression.

- **Catch the editor's attention:** Once you have your idea and the necessary contact info, it is time to put together an e-mail to entice the editor to sit up and take notice. Use a catchy title for the e-mail so it will stand out in the hundreds (maybe even thousands) he or she receives in a day.

- **Keep it short and simple:** Offer a very quick introduction, including a small taste of your credentials. This is not the place to write long prose; editors don't have time to read long-winded submissions. Keep your initial contact e-mail fewer than six sentences, just enough to give the editor an idea of why you are reaching out to him or her. If the editor is interested, you will get an e-mail back asking for more information.
- **Don't give up:** Don't be too shy to contact an editor more than once; just don't wear him or her out with daily e-mails. If you e-mail an editor and never get a reply, wait a few weeks and try again. Also try multiple publications, but don't pitch the same products or ideas to several at once, because they all want original content. If you send five magazines the same idea and three of them want to follow up, you'll have to disappoint two editors to make one happy.
- **If you're shy, start small:** Want to build up some credentials so you have some experience? Start with a small local newspaper. Newspaper staffs have been radically chopped in recent years, so they are begging for good content, especially when it's free. Little local newspapers generally have editors who are frequently in the office, so make a quick phone call to see if they accept articles. You might be surprised at how easy it is to land a feature in your local newspaper.

Magazine features are so much stronger than paid advertisements because they are the reason people buy or subscribe to the magazine. You don't have to choose the most famous publications to get the best results. Often, smaller niche magazines might be a better fit if your product has a very specific ideal customer.

Etsy Tip

Don't worry too much about pitching to every magazine you can find. Instead, concentrate on one or two a month. Each time you become published, it adds to your credibility when reaching out to the next editor.

Being Highlighted through Etsy

Most Etsy sellers dream of two Etsy milestones: being on the front page or being featured in the daily shopping newsletter. Instead of telling you things to do that might or might not work, I'm going to tell you my story of what I believe helped me land in the coveted Etsy Finds newsletter more than a dozen times and on the Etsy front page nearly twenty times, all within one year.

I learned very early on in blogging that the key to building relationships with others online was to leave comments. I started by leaving comments on my favorite blogs, ones that were honest and related to the content, in an authentic voice that had nothing to do with promoting myself. I would visit dozens of blogs every day, leaving thoughtful comments as often as I could. Leaving a comment on a blog is like reaching out to say hello to people who might feel like they are talking to an empty room. Speaking up and talking to bloggers through comments helped me find my place within the blogging world. I formed friendships through commenting that are still with me to this day, including some of my very closest friends.

When I began my Etsy shop, I knew I had to reach out to the handmade community and make myself known. I started out in the Etsy forums (which have been replaced with team message boards) talking to other sellers who were struggling with the same issues I had, ones that my everyday, real-life friends just didn't completely understand. It helped me to not feel so alone when I was spending twelve hours a day working on products and self-promoting my shop. I would rejoice with those lucky individuals who shared their success of landing on the front page or in that day's shopping newsletter to the Etsy community.

My very first front-page feature was pure luck, which is how most people wind up on the much-coveted main page of Etsy, because it can land you a ton of exposure to thousands of people in the forty-five or so minutes you are live. I almost didn't catch it; one of my blogging friends saw the front page and sent me a message on Twitter to hurry up and look. I knew I had gotten several orders back to back, which was highly unusual, but I didn't think too much about it and chalked it up to luck.

Yes, my first time was luck, but it made me hungry to figure out how to get even more exposure through the Etsy staff. First, I worked on my photographs. My original listings were full of horrible photos, so I made it my mission to take beautiful, high-quality photographs that Etsy's editorial staff would be comfortable promoting. I paid close attention to the shops that were being featured, dissecting their work to learn from the successful sellers. After I made my photographs look better, I thought really hard about how to be seen more.

Etsy editors are writers who produce content for the Etsy blog, so essentially they are bloggers. Bloggers love comments, especially when they are honest, authentic comments that add value to the conversation. Armed with that knowledge, I made it a priority to read the Etsy blog every day, and if I felt like I could comment with a real reply, I would leave a comment on the posts.

At first, I did this on basically any blog post, and then I decided to be a little choosier about which writers I was looking for. I started focusing on writers only if I could see my brand becoming part of their posts. There were only a couple who meshed well with my particular style, but I actively tried to learn more about those writers.

Writers on Etsy all have profiles, and many of them run shops themselves. Because Etsy makes it so easy to connect your Twitter and Facebook pages to your shop, I could easily find the writers on social media and follow them. No one uses social media to just talk out loud to themselves (and you shouldn't, either), so when these writers would ask questions, sometimes I would reply. I didn't intend to form solid relationships with them; I just wanted to make them aware of my brand. I tried not to be a stalker, but I offered natural reactions to whatever they shared, building an honest interest in them and their brands.

Within a couple of months, I landed a spot in my first Etsy Finds newsletter, which goes out to several hundred thousand users every day. In one day, from one newsletter mention, I received nearly one hundred orders. I had one hundred chances to make a great first impression on customers who had never seen my shop before, one hundred opportunities to turn those people into repeat customers. More than 10 percent of the people who ordered that day eventually returned to purchase with me again.

In the months that followed, I was featured in the newsletter a dozen-plus times, most of which meant lots of sales to new customers. Each and every time was a blessing, which I was extremely thankful for because, without them, my shop might not have become so successful. It brought my tiny handmade shop before hundreds of thousands of people, many of whom were ideal customers who might not have found me any other way.

If I hadn't decided to immerse myself in the Etsy community, I might never have been found in the sea of sellers. There are fifteen million handmade listings on Etsy on any given day, so the thirty or so featured in the daily newsletter have to be something special. I'm thankful that Etsy found me special, but I also feel that making sure my brand was visible to the people who curate those collections was a key to being seen. Building awareness of my brand was the ultimate goal, one that served me well.

A year or so after I found success on Etsy, I was invited to speak at my first blogging conference, teaching others to sell handmade goods. While the price of the conference was covered, there were other expenses I had to pay out of pocket. I knew it would be great exposure for my shop, but I wanted to see if I could find a sponsor to help offset the cost of the conference. Through a contact e-mail address I found on the site, I sent Etsy an e-mail and offered to write a post for their blog on the conference and promote them at the conference if they would cover some of my expenses.

In the e-mail, I explained how, thanks to Etsy, I was able to quit my day job within one year of opening my shop. I thought it would make me a great candidate to help spread the word to other conference attendees, many of whom were moms (like me) wanting to sell their handmade goods. Although Etsy didn't take me up on the initial request to sponsor me at the conference, they did respond to my e-mail.

About twice a week, Etsy writes a story about one of its sellers in a series, appropriately called "Quit Your Day Job." Whoever read the e-mail about the conference thought my story would be a great candidate for the series, so a writer contacted me to get more information. After I shared my whole story of how I successfully replaced my full-time income thanks to Etsy sales, they invited me to be part of the series. Sharing my story helped inspire other moms who wanted to pursue a similar path, and once again it put my shop in front of thousands of new fans, as the story was featured in the popular Etsy Seller newsletter.

Each time I was featured on Etsy, it helped to build my brand. There are other ways to be seen on Etsy, even if it's not through the editorial staff. Members create treasuries that include products from shops found all across the site. Each of the thirty front-page collections seen each day are pulled directly from the treasuries feature on Etsy. If you like pulling together collections, you can try to make your own so you can feature the work of others. Some sellers have a lot of fun shopping around and creating a treasury, hoping it will eventually end up on the front page.

Besides treasuries, you can also find communities full of teams for every medium, style, or location on the map, all through the Etsy Street Team feature. Team members frequently share advice and expertise, and they help promote each other. The support from teams is incredible, much like the forums were in the early years of Etsy. If you feel like you need some support, finding a team is the easiest way to fit in on Etsy.

08 | Financial Management

Business articles are full of scary statistics, usually claiming that 95 percent of small businesses fail within the first five years, mostly because of financial issues. There are lots of factors that go into the success or failure of any business, and Etsy shops are not exempt from the fundamental issues that plague other small businesses. Learning from the mistakes of those who have tried and failed in building their businesses is essential if you plan on withstanding the test of time and running a shop for years to come.

While some shop owners never intend for their shop to become their job for the rest of their lives, they still need to know the basic building blocks of how to make a profit and create a financially viable venture. To understand how to make money, you have to know what you have spent on every expenditure, right down to the very last business card. On top of learning where your business spends its money, you also have to look ahead to build in money for growth, without which your business can never expand.

Creative minds don't typically like to be bothered with numbers, sales statistics, or other such pragmatic things; we just want to make pretty stuff. Making a business out of making beautiful things is a fun idea, but you're going to have to wrap your mind around the numbers or you will sink your business. Barely skating by recouping the cost of making your products isn't a great way to build a business, but it is definitely a recipe for losing one. Handmade business owners can successfully make products and make money at the same time, but you must account for all the tiny details that the other 95 percent of businesses overlook.

Finding Hidden Costs

"Oh, that'll only take a minute, so I'm not factoring it into my price," is the death cry of thousands of Etsy shops. Equally destructive is, "Well, it will only cost a little bit, so I'll just take it out of my profits." Why are these two lines of logic so horrible? Because you will probably have twenty things that "only take a minute" to add value to your business, all of which you should be getting paid to do. There are so many aspects of running any business, most of which are typically delegated to an entire staff in a large corporation, but small business owners have to take the whole burden on themselves.

Chapter 5 included a thorough breakdown of all of the aspects of a product, all of which will affect prices, but there are some other business items in the background of your business that should be considered when figuring out the prices for your products. Not only will you need to make time to tend to each of these items (some much more frequently than others), taking your time seriously is the mark of a smart business owner. Brushing off the idea of being paid to do the work is a disastrous attitude to apply to your business.

Besides the time costs of filing paperwork and handling the business administration of your shop, you may also forget some simple expenses:

- **Taxes:** They're the nemesis of most creative minds, because punching numbers isn't necessarily the right brain's idea of a fun time. Even if you hire an accountant, you will still need to spend time gathering up receipts, paying invoices, and even paying yourself. Income taxes and property taxes must be filed in a timely fashion, and filling out the necessary paperwork or getting the information to your accountant will take a considerable amount of time. Depending on your tax bracket, you may have to pay as much as 40 percent of your profits to income tax alone. If you're charging only $10 an hour for labor, you'll be making less than minimum wage after taxes.

- **Retirement:** Unless you plan on working long past your golden years, you will need to put something away for the future. Let's call it an investment in your future time. Putting back part of your profits into your retirement plan might not be necessary, but most people will need to set aside a portion of their income to plan for their later years in life.

- **Insurance:** I know we've already discussed finding insurance, but if you do need it for your business, you need to be sure the premiums are included in your prices. In the beginning it may be hard to determine how much you need to add to your overall price to cover insurance, but after a while you will learn your average sales numbers and be able to divide the sales by your premium to factor the cost into your price.

- **Improving efficiency:** Efficiency engineers study companies to learn how to make their processes faster, which can increase profits by increasing the amount of product that can be made and decreasing the time it takes to do it. You may need to purchase tools to make your shop run faster or even plan to reorganize your studio to make it run faster.

- **Updating listings:** Products that sell frequently can become the cornerstones of your product line. The more of these items you create, the better they will become. We learn to fine-tune products through repetition. If you take a photo of an item, then make it a few hundred times over the course of six months, you will need to update your photos to reflect the very best version of your product. Skills improve, materials may be upgraded, or maybe your process changes slightly. In any case, you'll need to take fresh photographs so your shop stays as up to date as possible. Taking those new photos takes time, just as taking the originals did.

- **Travel costs:** At the very least, you will need to purchase fuel to shop for materials, but vintage sellers might scour the globe to find the very best wares. Some shop owners attend conferences or trade shows to help their businesses grow. Gas, airfare, hotels, booth fees, conference tickets, and even food while traveling for your business are all part of the costs you'll need to add to your prices if these expenditures are essential to your business.

- **Building in discounts:** At some point you're going to run a sale or promotion. Shops can help ease slow sales months by offering customers an incentive to buy, or simply as a reward for being valued customers. If you don't add a little padding to your price, you'll be taking a cut of your labor fees for those discounts.

By no means is this a completely exhaustive list, because smart business owners will find ways to think outside the box to promote their shops. The main point is to think beyond the brass tacks figures to come up with your product prices and include some wiggle room for all those other costs customers don't even think about. Unless you plan for them, those hidden fees will eat up all your profits, tearing your business down instead of building it up. You need to grow with time, not struggle to keep up.

Example: Pillow with a predicted price of $28.

Supplies	$5.85	$ 5.85	
Etsy fee	20 cents + 3.5 per-cent	$ 1.18	
PayPal fee	40 cents + 3.5 per-cent	$ 1.38	
Taxes	+10 percent	$ 2.80	
Retirement	+5 percent	$ 1.40	
Insurance	+3 percent	$ 0.84	
Discounts	+10 percent	$ 2.80	
Growth	+5 percent	$ 1.40	
	Total:	$17.65	Profit of $10.35

Reducing Costs by Growing Larger

As your shop grows larger, you'll start to build up capital (or, at least, you should). This will enable you to grow from a tiny start-up to a thriving small business. Some of the changes you make will decrease production time, while others will directly affect the cost of supplies, both of which will have a positive impact on your profit margin. If you never make changes, you will never grow.

Learning to make the most of your growth budget can change the direction of your business. The key is to test your decisions by starting small and thinking through each choice to be sure it's the next logical move to enhance your shop.

■ **Upgrade your supplies:** Choosing cheaper supplies might seem like a great financial move, but you may want to reconsider. Not only will higher-quality supplies add value to your product, you will find better results in the production time, too. There's nothing worse than fighting with cheap thread, resulting in an hour-long battle to create a product that normally takes fifteen minutes to make. Buying the best supplies you can afford is a smart move; as you can afford to invest in the next level up, you'll find your job gets easier. As you increase your productivity, you'll also increase your profits.

- **Upgrade your tools:** Beginning sellers might start by working with tools they acquired while pursuing their craft as a hobby, back when they didn't need to purchase the absolute best money could buy. When you can upgrade your tools, you'll also be able to speed up your production. Higher-level tools might work faster than their hobby-geared counterparts. For instance, an automated wood routing machine can definitely work faster than manually cutting out pieces with a scroll saw. A larger kiln can hold more pottery than a tiny one. In addition to producing greater volumes, better tools generally require less maintenance than cheaper ones, saving you downtime.

- **Buy larger quantities:** After running a shop for a few months or even a few years, you'll begin to know how much of certain supplies you use. You may need only one small package per month of something at first, and then as your product begins to sell, you may need ten or twenty packages a month. If you can buy larger quantities from wholesale sources, you'll usually spend much less on those supplies than you would on smaller quantities.

- **Anticipate your customers' needs:** When I started my own shop, I tried many different colors and patterns to see what would sell, because I really didn't know what colors would be the best to offer. Over time, I learned that my customers (like me) loved aqua. After a few months of paying attention to bestsellers, I knew when I created a new product the first color to try was any shade of aqua. When I decided to delve more into a varied palette of colors and patterns of fabric to use on pillow covers and table runners, I could spot a good aqua a mile away. Mostly it was gut instinct, because I listened to my customers who were in love with the beach-inspired shade. When I tried to venture out and try something new, I never had the same success rate. When I shopped specifically for my customers, giving them all sorts of aqua, I always did much better. Buying busy patterns and bright primary colors usually resulted in a waste of money. Cutting out bad decisions and fine-tuning my shop with my customer in mind helped me get more sales and grow my profits.

- **Hire some help:** Business is booming, and you're receiving more orders than you could possibly handle along with everything else you have on your plate. Looks like it's time to hire some help! You can go two different routes: a studio assistant or a virtual assistant. Studio assistants can help you to speed up your process by doing things like prep work, finishing, packing and shipping, or helping with production. Virtual assistants can help handle e-mail or work on your social media and marketing. Paying an assistant a portion of your labor fee will allow you to get more accomplished in a day, allowing you to keep up with orders or push your business to grow even more.

- **Continue your education:** Learning new skills for your craft can help in multiple ways. You can work faster or improve the level of your goods (which will be reflected in a higher price). You can also learn basic maintenance skills for tools that need regular care; doing it yourself can save a lot of money in the long run. Improving your photography skills can make your listings more appealing, helping them sell better. There is always something new to learn, and your shop will only improve as you educate yourself.

Business owners who strive to propel themselves and their businesses for growth will find better results than those who never try to move forward. Putting positive effort into your business will almost always yield positive results. Carefully plan out the steps you want to take, work toward them by setting goals, and you'll enjoy the benefits in your bottom line.

Taxes and Accounting

When I speak to people about selling on Etsy, one of the most frequent questions I get asked is, "What's your advice for taxes?" I always answer with the same three words: "Hire an accountant." With the hundreds of decisions you have to make on any given day, worrying about taxes isn't something you need to add to your plate. While it's absolutely possible to do your own accounting work, there's a peace of mind that comes from having an experienced accountant on your side. Any time you are hiring help, you want to find someone who will help make your business run easier, not create headaches and chaos.

What are your certifications?

Which license do you hold?

Where did you receive your education?

How much experience do you have?

What is your tax specialty?

Do you do all your own work, or do you outsource some services?

How long do you expect it to take to file my taxes?

What are your fees? Do you charge by the job or by the hour?

Do you have a privacy policy?

Five Tips to Help Find the Right Accountant

1. **Determine what you need:** Accountants can help in many aspects of your business, so you need to decide up front what you need help with so you can find the proper accountant. If you only need your taxes filed, you may not need to dig as deep to find the perfect person. However, if you intend to use your accountant to help with monthly bookkeeping, payroll, or other needs, you need to be a little more selective. You want to find someone you trust, because this person will be responsible for the financial well-being of your business.

2. **Ask for recommendations:** If you're a member of a guild or group that supports people in your field, usually someone will have a lead on a good accountant. Using your networking resources to find an accountant will help you find someone who will understand all the issues you are likely to face when it comes time to file your taxes. You can also ask family and friends to help find a reliable, experienced person and schedule an appointment so you can interview the accountant before deciding.

3. **Interview the accountant:** Choosing an accountant is about finding someone you can trust with your private financial matters. Question accountants to see if they have worked with others in your field, if they understand your situation, and if their personality is compatible with your own. (For more questions, see the Accountant Questionnaire worksheet.)

4. **Ask for references:** Good accountants should have no problem sharing the name of a few clients who will give you a better feel for the accountant. Ask them if their taxes were handled properly, if the work was done in a timely manner, and if they were happy with the results of their tax returns.

5. **Inquire about fees:** Talking about money isn't always the easiest thing to do, but the whole point of an accountant is to help you handle your money. An accountant who barely charges more than minimum wage probably isn't the person you want to trust with your business. You may not need the most expensive person, either. Choose someone who fits your budget, but also one who can handle your business needs.

Call it karma, the golden rule, or just doing the right thing—however you label it, one thing is clear: Running an ethical business is never a bad idea. Keeping a simple goal of being honest and fair to customers, other sellers, or anyone else you might interact with will only help your business in the long run. Occasionally the lines can be blurry, but if you are intentionally trying to make ethical choices, any minor slipups will be forgivable. We are all human, after all.

Legal matters are a completely different story. As a business owner, it is your job to know the legal issues pertaining to your business, because ignorance of the law is no excuse. You need to understand which ordinances and laws affect you in every aspect of your business, because you are the responsible party if things go awry.

Being Your Original, Awesome Self

Pinterest makes borrowing ideas way too easy, and unfortunately people do it way too often. In a world full of knockoffs from every major retailer, it's important that you stay true to yourself and your brand and be an original. While you may appreciate the style of a certain major brand, don't make a knockoff. You are the only person who can be you—so be the best one you can possibly be. Being yourself will help you to stand out in a crowd of shop owners who are simply trying to re-create items they've seen in catalogs.

While it's important to stay on top of trends, or even to use other brands for inspiration, do your own thing. It's already too hard to stand out in the sea of other handmade shops, so being unique isn't only ethical, it is vital to making your business last over the years.

On the flip side of the coin, with success you will find others who copy your ideas and designs. Hard as it might be, you have to stay calm. There are levels of idea theft, some outright and others overt. Either way, you have to carefully investigate the situation before deciding which action you need to take.

- **Items are very, very similar:** Sometimes in life, people just have similar ideas. If you take a set of similar popular supplies and put them in front of two people who both share the same style and product range, you will most likely come up with some similar product. As long as they are marketing the product in their own way, their brand is truly authentic to them, and they don't have twenty similar items to yours, then it's probably just a coincidence. Don't take it too personally. It's happened to everyone at some point.

- **Another seller has exact replicas of your products:** Honestly, it's a horrible feeling when you stumble upon a shop (or are alerted to it by friends/followers) that sells an item identical to yours. First, look to see when the seller began selling the items. You can browse through the person's sold listings to see exactly when the items sold. If you were selling the identical items a year before the seller in question was, politely send a message to ask that he or she remove the items. Unless you have patented your ideas (see patent information later in chapter), you can send a cease and desist letter, but only if the item is so original to you that no one else could have created it all on his or her own.

- **Your photographs or words are stolen:** Unlike ideas, words and photographs do have a copyright. If you can prove you published the works before anyone else, you have copyright protection. First, send a cease and desist letter telling the person that if he or she does not remove your photos or writing, you will hand the situation over to your lawyer. (We'll talk more about copyright later.)

Etsy Tip

Watermarking photographs with your logo will help to prevent theft.

Most sellers are honest and have no intentions of stealing your ideas or content. A minute group of sellers who don't care to do things by the book are setting up highly illegal shops whose items violate Etsy policy. Each page has a place to report the shop or item if you believe the seller is blatantly going against policy or is selling something illegal.

Trademarks, Patents, and Copyrights

Running any profitable business means you have to protect what you build. Trademarks, patents, and copyright laws all serve different functions to protect your brand, your products, and the imagery and wording you use to represent your brand. Because you're running an online business, it is absolutely crucial that you understand the steps to protect yourself.

- **Trademarks protect your brand:** To gain a trademark, you must apply for any portion of your business branding identity you wish to protect, one by one. Names, symbols, logos, taglines, and even a jingle made specifically for your business can be trademarked. Applying online is easy at www.USPTO.gov, or this can be handled through an attorney. Before filing, you can search the United States Patent and Trademark Office (USPTO) website for anyone else using the name or portion of your business you wish to trademark. If your application is accepted and you are granted a trademark, you can legally protect your business name or other trademarked properties from being used by others. Of course, to take legal action against another business means that you will accrue legal fees, but some instances may demand action.

- **Patents protect newly invented products or ideas:** Basic products that are already in existence can be patented only if you have a brand-new formula that drastically changes the overall product. If you are developing a product from scratch that has never been made before, you can apply for a patent to protect your idea. Patents can also be applied for through the USPTO website. As with trademarks, you have to be legally prepared to defend your patent if you can prove someone has stolen your idea.

- **Copyrights protect intellectual property:** According to the US Copyright Office, those properties include "literary, dramatic, musical, and artistic works, such as poetry, novels, movies, songs, computer software and architecture. Copyright does not protect fact, ideas, systems, or methods of operation, although it may protect the way these things are expressed." As far as an Etsy shop is concerned, if you create the original wording and photographs for your products, they are protected by copyright. You can legally apply for a copyright with the United States Copyright Office (www.copyright.gov), but if you can successfully prove you created the words or photograph, you legally own those properties even without a formal copyright on file.

Because your business is worth protecting, you should take note of the proper steps to take through the proper channels. Do not be afraid to defend those legal channels you set up, because it is your duty as a trademark, patent, or copyright holder to ensure others do not use your material. Typically, a simple e-mail can solve most matters, because many times a business owner simply makes the mistake of choosing the same business name you do. However, if someone blatantly steals your brand or ideas, you need to follow through with a cease and desist notification. Past that point, you will need an attorney to help with legal matters. (You can find tips on finding a lawyer later in this chapter.)

On the other hand, if you are the offender, Etsy can—and will—shut down your shop if you do not comply with the appropriate laws. If it is truly a mistake, you will most likely have plenty of time to make the necessary changes, but usually a violation is a simple matter of not looking to see if someone else is using a brand or product name. Just look around to be sure no one else has already protected the name or product in question to be safe.

Copyrighted Supplies

Just as you want to protect your copyrighted materials, so do the creators of copyrighted supplies. Fabric stores frequently carry bolts of fabric that are printed with trademarked and copyrighted characters and logos. Those fabrics are not typically legal to use to create items to sell. Disney, along with other companies, are highly protective of their properties (as they should be) and will not tolerate sellers who use those protected images.

Of course, fabric is not the only protected medium. Song lyrics are notoriously used for everything from artwork to clothing; however, legally the copyright holder of the song owns all rights to those words. You can use simple phrases, even if they appear in songs, such as "I love you" or "happy birthday," but if you are taking entire lines from a song, it's illegal to do so without written permission from the rights holder. (Note: This often involves a fee.)

Quotes, however, are a different story. Famous quotes can be used, as long as you give the author credit somewhere on the piece, and you do not use his or her likeness to sell the particular item. Using an image of a famous person (e.g., Audrey Hepburn) is not legal because you are using the face of a person. Simply quoting words from a famous person is usually covered by the First Amendment, but should you have any questions on the matter, please seek legal advice.

Children's Items

Etsy sellers who sell children's items of any kind need to be aware of the Consumer Product Safety Improvement Act (CPSIA), which mandates all aspects of items intended for children younger than age twelve. The laws are quite comprehensive and cover everything from clothes to toys to home decor—anything marketed for a child younger than twelve years of age.

Controlled by the Consumer Product Safety Commission, the laws affect Etsy sellers who produce any children's goods. As of 2009, the act limits levels of components such as lead, phthalates, and small parts. The act lists a complete selection of materials that can be used without testing; however, if your business uses any parts not covered by the approved materials, you must have your products individually tested and labeled before selling them.

If your business sells products intended for children, be very careful to comply with all of the rules and regulations mandated by CPSIA.

Hiring an Attorney

Small business owners can have varied needs when it comes to hiring an attorney. You need to find someone who can help guide you through the legalities of running your business—everything from trademarks to liability lawsuits. Most Etsy shop owners rarely need a lawyer, but it's good to have someone on call in case issues arise. Finding the right attorney for your business can be an unnerving process, but if you follow some basic guidelines, you can find the best person for the job (see sidebar).

Zoning: Can You Start at Home?

Local zoning laws in every district have two main areas: residential and commercial. Because your home-based business will most likely be in a residential area, you need to contact your local zoning office to learn how this affects your business. Zoning laws are different in every area, but most have regulations on what types of

Finding the Right Attorney

- **Look for experience:** If you are just starting a business, you want to find an attorney who has enough experience to help you understand what your business needs to do, legally speaking. Over time, an experienced attorney can do more than just file paperwork; he or she can help to defend your brand and business for long-term success.

- **Listen for communication cues:** Seek out a lawyer who can talk to you at your level. If the person is spouting off legal terms and doesn't stop to help you understand the process, you may want to keep looking for a better match.

- **Determine availability:** Take note of how long it took you to get a consultation appointment. If it took a long time, that's a good indicator that the person is too busy to handle your needs. Ask how quickly the attorney responds to clients, because you need to know that your attorney can promptly handle any situation that may arise.

- **Ask for references:** Although attorneys can't disclose certain attorney/client relationships, any attorney should be able to provide at least a few references. Follow through and see how many of those references are still clients and if they are happy with the services.

- **Get rates in writing:** Before you make your final decision, make sure you know how much the services will cost. Attorney fees range from $50 an hour to thousands of dollars per hour, so be sure you can afford the person's expertise.

businesses can be run in which zones. Permits may be required in some areas. Be sure to talk to your local zoning office to ensure you are in compliance.

Etsy Fees

The Etsy policy clearly states, "You may not use Etsy to direct shoppers to another online selling venue to purchase the same items as listed in your Etsy shop, as this may constitute fee avoidance. This includes posting links/URLs or providing information sufficient to locate the other online venues."

Avoiding Etsy fees by rerouting customers denies the website its portion of the sale, which Etsy has earned by bringing the customer to your shop through a search. With millions of users, Etsy has overhead and employees to pay, so you are essentially hurting its business if you avoid the fees.

While most shop owners would never think to do such a thing, be aware that if you are caught, your shop can be closed permanently. As with all ethical issues, just do the right thing and you'll have no worries.

Giving Back

Ethical issues aside, giving to charity just feels good. Shop owners often run some type of promotional aspect of their business, whether it is a specific item or a portion of their overall sales, geared toward giving to charity. Although giving to charity isn't mandatory for Etsy shop owners, it can help your customers see an altruistic side of your business that may appeal to them. With that said, looking good shouldn't be the reason you donate.

Sellers across the spectrum find reasons dear to their hearts and reach out with charitable donations from their profits. Small shops starting out may not have the resources to donate financially, so they find ways to donate their time to help charitable organizations. Almost any type of seller can find ways to help a charity through his or her shop.

- **Bath and beauty sellers:** Goods could be donated to homeless shelters, because everyone needs good skin care.
- **Home decor shops:** Donations of blankets or pillows would help homeless shelters, too.
- **Jewelry makers:** Special pieces could be created to symbolize traumatic events and a portion of the profits given to relief organizations.
- **Supply sellers:** Surplus goods could be donated to schools for their arts and crafts programs.
- **Pet goods shops:** A portion of profits or some products could be supplied to animal shelters.

The range of good deeds that can be accomplished by affiliating your shop with a specific charity is endless. Paying a good deed forward is just another way to put a positive outlook on your shop, and this will only boost your motivation to run an outstanding enterprise.

10 | Thinking Long Term

You've learned how to create and run your Etsy shop from the ground up. You know all about branding, marketing, bookkeeping, SEO, photography, customer service, shipping, and all the minutiae that will make your business run smoothly from start to finish. It's only appropriate to contemplate: Where is the finish line?

How long you truly see yourself running an Etsy shop depends on how you choose to utilize it. Just as no two businesses are the same, no two answers will be the same for this question. Every person needs different things from his or her business, so you should consider the end goal of your shop. If you are building up cash for a down payment on a home, running your shop as a side business for a while during the savings period makes sense. Many people run the business to help cover college expenses while their children are finishing their education. Others might want to run a shop only long enough to build up a local clientele. If your goal is short term, will you run your shop after you've met your goal?

Some artisans decide to create businesses that will grow through time with hopes of handing them down to their children one day. They start a shop and run it for several years, with no plans to stop until retirement. That's a great plan, but you're going to need to set goals to ensure you can attain that kind of longevity.

No matter what your choice is, let's be clear: Your shop's duration is in your hands. There's no expiration date, no one to pull the plug but you. Deciding how long you want to run your shop will help you make decisions such as upgrading equipment, how much to spend on marketing, or even how much to invest in supplies. If your goal is to run a short-term shop to meet specific financial goals, you may not need top-of-the-line equipment with a hefty price tag. Mid-grade equipment will most likely handle the demands of a shop intended to run for a set number of years.

Building a business to last for the long term means making smarter investments, not only in equipment but also in terms of time. Running a long-term business is a marathon, not a sprint. You want to attract customers and turn them into people who will shop with you for years and years, not just once or twice. Even long-term businesses can have different goals—either keeping a small, intimate business or growing to be recognized as a larger brand.

Staying Small

Business owners come in a variety of sizes, including small, boutique shops that remain intimate and relaxed. While you can run a successful shop with almost any type of product, if your goal is to stay small and devote only a few hours a week to your business, you'll need to think about how to keep your business within your comfort zone.

Keeping a business small requires much less energy, resources, and, most of all, time. Running any business can eat up more hours in the day than meets the eye, but smaller shops require much less attention. If maintaining a small shop is your goal, you need to assess carefully how much time you have to put into your shop and what you truly need to achieve, and set your goals accordingly. When you're clear on your business goals, you will know how to make decisions regarding growth and upcoming opportunities. If your time is limited, don't spread yourself too thin—only you know how much time you want to devote to your shop. Once you have your business up and running, there are a few ways you can slow down the stream of work if you find it becomes overwhelming:

- **Say no to custom work:** Working with customers on highly personalized orders takes a lot of extra energy. Turning down custom orders may seem like a bad business move, but it could be even worse if you agree to a large order and then have trouble fulfilling it. Politely tell inquiring customers that you cannot accept custom work at the moment, and pass along the name of a trusted competitor (yes, you can find one). If the customer is persistent and you decide to take the custom order, give that person a time frame that will allow you plenty of room to work it into your schedule. Although it may seem outrageous, I've had customers wait as long as two months to get a custom order fulfilled because they specifically wanted me to do the work. If you do have an extended timetable, be sure to communicate clearly with your customer regarding schedule.

- **Slow down your social media:** If you can understand the importance of social media marketing, you'll also know that less marketing can mean less traffic. This isn't a surefire solution, but slowing down your marketing efforts can reduce the flow of traffic coming into your shop. While you may not be able to completely control the traffic, if you are facing an influx of orders, you may want to pull the reins on any future marketing efforts you haven't released yet, such as upcoming newsletters. Because sharing your goods on social media outlets can be highly effective, you can also limit your exposure by simply doing less.

- **Reduce your inventory:** When you are working to grow your shop, one of the main things you can do to activate growth is to increase the number of products you carry. Less inventory helps to avoid overselling. The fewer items you carry, the fewer the opportunities your customers have to stumble upon your shop and make a purchase. Start by reducing your not-so-great-selling items—those products you might like but are rarely or never purchased. After you have culled the weaker products from your line, if you are still out-selling your goals, next take away pieces you don't love to make. Don't be ashamed—everyone has them. Slowly take them out of your line until you start to have control over your orders.

- **Raise your prices:** If you've reduced your marketing, turned down custom orders, and thinned out your product line, yet you *still* have too much business, it's time to raise your prices. If you are selling more than you can handle, then your time is more valuable and you should be charging appropriately. Raising your prices may deter new customers, but be careful not to alienate your tried-and-true repeat customer base. Don't price gouge your customers; instead, try raising rates in small increments until you have found a price that allows you to handle your business comfortably. (Bonus: You'll need fewer sales to meet your financial sales goals!)

- **Put your shop on vacation:** This is a last-resort tactic, as it affects your SEO and your customers. It will stop all sales. Choosing vacation mode for your Etsy shop will hide all active listings from customers, so no one will be able to purchase from your shop. Mostly people use this mode for vacation time, illness, or other extended periods when they cannot accept orders. Some shop owners will occasionally use vacation mode to halt sales and catch up on existing orders. Please know that when you do reopen your shop, it will take several days for Google and other search engines to begin showing your shop in their search results, leading to a few extra days of slower than normal sales. If you truly have more business than you can handle, or you just need to take a couple of weeks away from your shop, vacation mode is the best choice.

Growing Your Shop Larger

Want to grow your business to be larger than you can handle alone? Maybe your goal is to create a full-time career and quit your day job. Or what if your goal is to grow larger and see your products sold in stores around the world? Welcome to the American dream! Hundreds of Etsy success stories can vouch for the fact that if you build something customers will buy, market it well, and provide excellent customer service, you can create a full-time business through Etsy. I'm not the only person out there who earns a full-time income selling handmade goods; there are thousands of sellers on the site who have made Etsy their full-time job, either in handmade, vintage, or selling supplies.

If your dream is to build a shop that generates a high enough profit margin to run your business full time, there is one major strategy you cannot neglect: Spend just as much time on the business end of your shop as you do the creative side. While artisans and crafters can get lost for hours in the creation of a product, they also need to look at their pieces as marketable goods that need to generate an income relative to their worth in terms of time and supplies. If you are selling items for a paltry sum of money only so you can rack up numbers on your sidebar, you're missing the point.

If you intend to run your shop for years to come, working full time selling goods, you need to think of yourself as a salesperson as much as you are a creator or curator. Putting effort into the sales end through SEO, photographs, descriptions, marketing, and bookkeeping will enable your business to progress fluidly throughout time. Don't waste your focus on selling only one item; instead, concentrate on selling your business as a whole. If you are working to bring customers into your shop, you are creating an experience. Once customers have a pleasant experience, they will be much more likely to return, giving you the coveted repeat business that is crucial for the longevity of your business.

Throughout this book, you've learned all the tools for growing your business, so putting them to use is now within your reach. The hard part is finding time to implement everything you possibly can to grow your business. Remember that slow and steady growth is much more important than rising to the top quickly. The months and years you spend growing your business sale by sale, customer by customer, will be the best option, rather than burning yourself out by trying to take on too much too quickly.

As your business reaches new levels each month or year, you'll start to learn from the things that did and didn't work. Over time, you'll be faced with opportunities, good and bad. It's not always easy to distinguish between the two. Some opportunities may look good before you get involved, but after crunching the numbers you may realize it's not such a great deal after all. You'll be presented with ways to advertise, receive requests from charity organizations needing donations, or get offers to be featured on websites or in print. Some are great, some are not. Often, an opportunity that shows great results for one shop will not work for another. Each time you make a decision, you'll learn a little more. Eventually you will be able to see up front which opportunities will work for your business and which ones won't. Be cautious not to sacrifice your business goals to accept opportunities because you may be scared of missing out. There's always another option.

Careful investing is another portion of sustaining a business for long-term growth. Of course, you'll want to invest to help your business grow, but choose solid reasons that fit your business needs, not just because it may or may not work. Investing a lot of money in a brand-new, untested product can be catastrophic for a small business owner. Wade slowly into huge decisions, and do not let your emotions control your thinking. While it may seem like a great investment for a potter to buy the biggest kiln she can find, her business could come to a halt if there isn't enough money left over to purchase supplies or electricity to run her equipment. Patience is a necessary virtue when it comes to upgrading. Choose wisely and at the right time.

If your decision is to grow as large as possible, eventually you're going to need some help. Hiring an assistant can be one of the best investments you can make in your business. Handing off bits of your work to someone else can make you more productive, not to mention push you further. When I hired my first assistant to help me with my workload, I realized that I pushed myself harder when working with her. I was paying her by the hour, so I wanted to get as much as I possibly could for my money. Because I was essentially giving someone else a portion of my pay, I had to streamline my methods to ensure I was more than making up for the loss of profits by creating more product than I could on my own.

Hiring Help

Once you have successfully grown your business past the point where you can handle it on your own, you may find that you need an assistant. It's a scary step, but finding the right assistant to do the right job can be a blessing for your business. It's no surprise that two people can do more than one, but you have to find the right person for the job.

Before you start taking applications or conduct any interviews, you need to know exactly what your new assistant will be doing. If you need someone who is a seamstress, you probably want to hire someone with extensive sewing experience. If you're looking for an organizational whiz, then make sure the candidate is qualified to help. Not all assistants need to do the same jobs (at one point I had three of them at once). You need to determine which parts of your business you can comfortably hand off to someone else so you can focus on the parts of your business that need your full attention. You don't have to hire someone to come in and help make product, though. You can find help in a variety of ways:

- **Hire an accountant:** We've already discussed bookkeeping, but hiring help with your paperwork is a smart move, especially if you're not particularly organized. From taxes to simple accounting, you can pay a reasonable rate for someone who will do your paperwork right, saving you not only time but often a lot of aggravation. If you're not great at tending to your own bookkeeping, paying someone a small monthly fee to take over the chore can be a great investment.

- **Outsource your marketing:** Virtual assistants are another resource for portions of your business that might eat up your time. Spending hours putting together graphics for e-mail promotions, sharing your shop through social media, or even fielding e-mails and questions that do not require your true attention are all parts of your business that are easy to delegate to someone else. Of course, you'll need to be sure anyone handing interaction with your customers is thoroughly trained and will show them the same level of customer service you demand, but finding the right person can help you focus on the important part of a creative business—creating.

- **Have someone do your shipping:** Most of the requirements to send products out the door are pretty cut and dried—the perfect task for an assistant to do. After an assistant learns your procedure for packing orders, where things are located, and how you handle the rest of your shop's shipping needs, it's a simple process for someone else to take over the job. If your assistant drives his or her own car to the post office, it might be an insurance issue, so check with your insurance agent to see if an assistant is covered driving your vehicle. If not, the postal service does offer pickup options that might help you eliminate a huge portion of your daily task list.

- **Find a hands-on helper:** An assistant who can help you with the actual production process is probably the hardest type of help to find, but it can yield the biggest rewards. Working side by side with someone on a regular basis means you want to find a helper with great skills and a great attitude. Even if you do not let the person make the actual product, an assistant can help in so many other ways. Setting up for work, such as getting out materials or tools, can take a lot of time, especially if you are using different supplies all day long. Your assistant can pull out the pieces you need and put them away after you're finished, saving you a lot of time and keeping you organized so that your studio runs more smoothly. If you are setting up and breaking down a small workspace several times a day for a variety of projects, the assistant can be very useful in making the transition time faster. Assistants who understand how your business works can help keep you on track with things like inventory, scheduling, or other tasks that can make your workday easier.

Learning what type of assistant your business needs to run better is the first step to hiring the right help. We've already discussed how to find an accountant, so let's look to the other types to see how to effectively find the right candidate for the job.

Choosing a Virtual Assistant

Virtual assistants are a great resource for online communication or transactions you need to tend to on a regular basis but can hand off to someone else. Many online retailers use them for things such as customer service, marketing, and even scheduling. The beauty of a virtual assistant is that he or she can live basically anywhere in the world and still do the work you need.

Hiring someone online is somewhat scary, which is why using a freelance service is a great option. My personal favorite resource for finding an online assistant is Elance.com (think "freelance" without the "fre"). The website connects people needing work with businesses looking to hire help, keeping both parties safe and secure.

You post a job opening, receive résumés (from all over the world), and choose the person to do the job for you. Elance also has a clock in and out system, complete with screenshots so you know when your assistant is working. You are billed the hours, pay through the site, and the freelancer receives his or her payment. The site is full of great freelance workers, including writers, photograph editors, and even marketing specialists. If you're looking to hire help through an online source, it's definitely a great option.

If you would rather have someone you know and can speak to personally, recommendations from friends can be a great way to go. I have a marketing assistant who lives near me, and an online friend from Texas hired her after I told her about the great work I received. It was a win-win, because not only could she do marketing work for me, she also does it for other clients and even cross-promotes each of her clients (upon approval) to the other channels she manages.

Choosing a Studio Assistant

Hiring help to work with you every day is a little harder than hiring someone to work online only. Not only do you need the person to do great work, you also need to find someone with a compatible attitude and personality for your business. Bringing someone into your own personal space is a little different from hiring someone outside your home. You need to trust your studio assistant not only with your business but also with access to your home.

> **Etsy Tip**
>
> Be sure your insurance covers anyone working in your home.

Reliability is also a huge factor. If you want to start your day at 8:00 a.m., you need to be sure your assistant will be there on time. If your hours are more flexible, you may need to find someone who can change his or her hours to fit your needs. Busy holiday seasons may require more hours in the day to cover all your sales, so if you need someone to help work those hours, make sure up front that your candidates can take on the extra time.

Name: _____

Date of birth: _____

Address: _____

_____

Phone number: _____

Education: _____

_____

_____

Employment history (last three jobs): _____

_____

_____

_____

_____

Special skills related to business: _____

_____

_____

Personal references: _____

_____

_____

Finding the right employee can be done in several different ways, but tradition-ally you can hire through these sources:

- **Local employment office:** Every area has a service to help unemployed peo-ple find work. These places are typically free of charge; however, some areas may ask a small administrative fee. This type of service will take in a huge number of applications, and you may have to go through hundreds of people before finding the right person for the job.
- **Temporary agencies:** If you need only seasonal help, temporary agencies can be useful because they will field applicants and present you with the best matches for your needs. Usually temporary agencies take out all taxes

and so forth, and you pay the agency directly for the employee. This type of employment isn't available in all areas, but it is a great option if you need only short-term help a few weeks out of the year.

- **Classifieds:** It may seem a little archaic to use a newspaper or local printed circular to find an employee for your online shop, but it's actually a great way to find a local assistant. Once again, you may field hundreds of applicants, but you can narrow the search by asking them to apply online or submit a résumé via e-mail.
- **Employment websites:** You can also find employees on employment websites like Monster.com or even Craigslist.org. Once again, you'll need to weed out all of the applicants who aren't right for the job, but using websites to find employees for an Internet-based business isn't a bad idea, because your employees will need to have basic knowledge of how the web works to apply for the job.

Once you've received applications, you're going to want to conduct interviews to narrow down the prospective people for the job. A two-interview process is a great way to really feel out the applicants and get a better understanding of who they are and how your personalities will mesh. After the first round of interviews, call back the best of the bunch for a second interview. Before the scheduling your second interview, check out all their references and call previous employers to verify their information is true.

Sample Interview Questions

Why do you want this type of job?

What are your outside interests?

Do you know about handmade goods/selling supplies/vintage resale?

What are your major weaknesses?

What are your best strengths?

How do you think others would describe you?

How do you feel you can contribute to my business?

Do you have any questions for me?

After you conduct the second set of interviews, if you are still not sure whom to choose between two or three applicants, ask them to spend a couple of hours in your studio to see if they can pick up on your method of working. There is nothing more frustrating than finding an assistant who looks great on paper and is nice to work with, yet cannot physically do the work you need. Having the candidates spend just a few hours working with you will help you determine whether or not they are truly a good fit for your business.

> **Etsy Tip**
>
> Contact your accountant to set up all the financial aspects of how to pay your employee, including tax withholding and Social Security payments.

Should You Stay on Etsy Forever?

Etsy is such a great place to open up an online business, but some small business owners think it may not be wise to stay on the website forever. Personally, I've tried other selling venues with little to no success; Etsy was always the best option for me to run my handmade business. The support system from the staff, experience from other sellers, and the customer base just cannot be replicated, no matter how hard other websites may try.

Not all small businesses have the same experience, though. Etsy can be used as a platform to start a business and grow it to the next level.

- **Selling exclusively through wholesale:** Many artisans start out with a small Etsy shop, using the time to build up the very best product line they can create. In their time there, sellers parlay their success by setting up wholesale accounts and selling exclusively to either boutique shops or even mass-market retailers like Anthropologie. While it does take a lot of work to get to that point, along with a substantial investment to support the volume of goods you need for the jump, Etsy sellers often realize their passion isn't in selling but in the creating. However, many of those same sellers would not have been discovered by larger companies if they hadn't first started on Etsy.

- **Jumping to your own website:** Because Etsy can bring in such a wealth of customers, sellers often begin their fan base on Etsy and later build their own websites, moving shop in the process. Even if you do decide to build your own website outside of your Etsy shop, keeping a line of goods listed on Etsy can bring you customers you may not have without it. Running two shops may seem a little overwhelming, but if you are selling the same items, it's really only a matter of a few extra clicks to send out orders.

- **Selling your business:** While it is against Etsy's Terms of Use to sell your Etsy shop to another person, you can sell your inventory, supplies, equipment, clientele list, experience, and all your marketing accounts. All of this information is vital to someone who wants to take the reins of an already thriving business. The other aspects of your business can be sold, but if the new owner chooses to remain on Etsy, he or she will need to open up a new shop, and you can send your customers there through your shop announcement after you close your shop.

Whether you choose to sell on the website for a short time or for the long term, Etsy is an amazing resource for any seller who wants to create a line of handmade goods, sell supplies, or curate a vintage shop. The sky is the limit when it comes to how far you can take your business on Etsy. Rob Kalin's vision has changed the handmade world, creating a viable way for people to make a living from selling their wares right out of their own home. Yes, there are a few rules to follow, but if you can navigate the website, find your place, market it well, and provide great customer support, you can build a thriving business using this platform.

Appendix A: Online Resources for Etsy Businesses

Etsy-Specific

Etsy
www.etsy.com

Craft Count
www.craftcount.com

Craft Cult
www.craftcult.com

Craftopolis
www.craftopolis.com

Everything Etsy
www.everythingetsy.com

Blogging

Blogger
www.blogger.com

WordPress
www.wordpress.com (free hosting)
www.wordpress.org (self-hosted)

Domain Purchasing and Website Hosting

Blue Host

www.bluehost.com

Phone: (888) 401-4678

Go Daddy

www.godaddy.com

Phone: (480) 505-8877

Host Gator

www.hostgator.com

Phone: (866) 96-GATOR / (866) 964-2867

E-mail Newsletter Services

Constant Contact

www.constantcontact.com

Phone: (866) 876-8464

iContact

www.icontact.com

Phone: (877) 820-7837

Mail Chimp

www.mailchimp.com

Employment Services

Career Builder

www.careerbuilder.com

Elance

www.elance.com

Monster (for employers)

hiring.monster.com

Financial

PayPal
www.paypal.com
Phone: (888) 221-1161

QuickBooks
www.quickbooks.com
Phone: (800) 683-3280

Fonts and Free Graphics

Fonts.com (free and paid fonts)
www.fonts.com

Font Squirrel (free commercial-use fonts)
www.fontsquirrel.com

Piddix
www.piddix.com/banners.htm

The Graphics Fairy (copyright-free graphics)
www.thegraphicsfairy.com

Photography Services and Editing

Flickr
www.flickr.com

Gimp
www.gimp.com

iPiccy
www.ipiccy.com

Photobucket
www.photobucket.com

Picasa
picasa.google.com

PicMonkey
www.picmonkey.com

Printing Services
Moo Cards
www.moo.com
Phone: (401) 680-4933

UPrinting
www.uprinting.com
Phone: (888) 888-4211

Vista Print
www.vistaprint.com
Phone: (866) 614-8002

Shipping
Federal Express
www.fedex.com
Phone: (800) GOFEDEX / (800) 463-3339

Stamps.com
www.stamps.com
Phone: (888) 434-0055

United Parcel Service
www.ups.com
Phone: (800) 782-7892

United States Post Office
www.usps.com
Phone: (800) 222-1811

SEO Tools

Google Analytics
www.google.com/analytics

Google Keyword Planner Tool
adwords.google.com/KeywordPlanner

Google Trends
www.google.com/trends

Social Media

Facebook
www.facebook.com

Google+
plus.google.com

Instagram
www.instagram.com

Pinterest
www.pinterest.com

Twitter
www.twitter.com

YouTube
www.youtube.com

United States Government

Internal Revenue Service
www.irs.gov

US Copyright Office
www.copyright.gov

Phone: (877) 476-0778 (toll free)
Library of Congress
Copyright Office
101 Independence Ave. SE
Washington, DC 20559-6000

US Patent and Trademark Office
www.uspto.gov
Phone: (800) 786-9199
USPTO Headquarters—Main Campus Address
Madison Buildings (East & West)
600 Dulany St.
Alexandria, VA 22314

US Small Business Administration
www.sba.gov
Phone: (800) 827-5722
US Small Business Administration
409 3rd St. SW
Washington, DC 20416

Additional Selling Websites
ArtFire
www.artfire.com

Big Cartel
www.bigcartel.com

Big Commerce
www.bigcommerce.com

StorEnvy
www.storenvy.com

Top Hatter
www.tophatter.com

Creative Conferences

Artful Business Conference
www.artfulbusinessconference.com

Craftcation
www.craftcationconference.com

Haven Conference
www.havenconference.com

SNAP
www.snapconference.com

Appendix B: Etsy Glossary

Admirers: Customers who love your shop and want to bookmark it for future use can "favorite" your shop, which makes them admirers or followers of your business.

Circles: The Etsy equivalent to adding a shop to your newsfeed, similar to other social media sites. When added to a circle, shoppers will see new items listed in your shop within their personal dashboard. (See also: **Followers.**)

Conversations/Convos: Etsy's e-mail system for private messages between two Etsy users.

Curator: Someone who puts together a collection of items from shops across Etsy into a treasury. (See also: **Treasury.**)

Dashboard: The back-end section of a shop, where all administrative functions occur within an Etsy shop.

Destash: Leftover supplies put together into a listing, usually for much less than the original retail price.

Dos and Don'ts: Etsy rules or terms of use are put together in this subsection of the website. This area lists every rule for buying and selling on Etsy.

Eatsy: A frequent type of feature post on the Etsy blog sharing recipes from around the world.

Etsy Ads: Purchase-based advertising available directly through Etsy that shows up randomly on the top of the page when customers search for items using keywords within your shop.

Etsy Checkout: Payment system that runs directly through Etsy, avoiding PayPal. Sellers are paid from Etsy for their orders, after a processing fee has been deducted.

Etsy Finds: A daily collection of goods curated by Etsy staff members (or invited guests). This is a free feature of Etsy and a highly coveted honor because staff members choose only the very best items to be featured in this daily blog post and e-mail, which is seen by millions.

Featured Seller/Shop: Etsy's blog regularly features the best sellers on the website in all three categories (vintage, supplies, and handmade).

Feedback: After a sale, both buyer and seller have an opportunity to leave an opinion on the transaction that is open to the public to see. The statistics from the positive, neutral, or negative feedback are all averaged out, giving the user a percentage rating with a maximum of 100 percent.

Flagging: Because of the strict nature of goods allowed to be sold on Etsy, there are times when items do not meet the requirements. Flagging is a way to let Etsy staff know that you believe an item to be the wrong fit for Etsy. If your item is wrongly flagged, Etsy staff will give you a chance to plead your case before permanently removing the questionable item.

Followers: Followers are the admirers of an Etsy shop—i.e., those who have put the shop's activity into their circle.

Front Page: Etsy's main page is a collection of goods found via the Treasury feature, which showcases the best of what Etsy has to offer. A front-page feature can bring a lot of traffic into a shop, so it is great exposure for any shop lucky enough to be singled out.

Hearts: "Favorites" were previously called "hearts" (and often still are by longtime users). This is the bookmarking feature to remember an Etsy item or shop.

Hotness: Treasuries are chosen for the front page by the number of views and clicks received. The more activity shown in a treasury, the higher the hotness.

Lookbook: A catalog style publication, either in print or online, which allows customers to see your products in a stylized setting. Usually published to announce new collections or for seasonal display.

One of a Kind (OOAK): Items made only once and never duplicated are tagged with this description so buyers will know it is a completely unique item and available one time only.

Online Labs: Etsy hosts webcasts on a variety of topics, ranging from business help to craft tutorials and other topics, all free on the Etsy website. These are generally open to viewer interaction and are sometimes streamed in real time.

Quit Your Day Job (QYDJ): Sellers who have successfully replaced their day jobs through selling on Etsy are sometimes featured in a story on the Etsy blog.

Relist: After an item has been purchased, sellers have the ability to offer a listing by making it available for sale again in their shops. Relisting an item currently in production is a shortcut versus writing an entirely new listing.

Renew: If an item has not sold in the four months allotted on Etsy, sellers can refresh the expired listing and make it available in their shops. Some sellers believe that renewing an item that has been sitting idle for a few weeks can bring in new customers, because renewing an item also makes it fresh in the circles of your followers.

Shop Announcement: Shop owners have a small section at the top of their shop pages to share important information with their customers. The space is great to use SEO keywords to maximize your shop's search engine appeal. There is a large amount of room, but the area has a drop-down box, so only a few lines at the top show immediately on the main page.

Shop Local: Customers who want to find items close to their geographical location can use this feature. It is also helpful to furniture sellers or makers of large items who do not wish to ship their goods and would rather make sales in their own area.

Teams/Street Teams: Groups of Etsy members with similar interests can gather in the Teams area of Etsy. Team Captains are the heads of the groups, followed by helpers who are Team Leaders; the rest are Team Members. Each team can set up its own page on Etsy, which includes a forum where members can communicate.

Treasury: Any Etsy member can put together a collection of twelve items with four hidden alternates. Treasuries are searchable, can be added to a favorites list, or even receive comments from viewers. The very best treasuries are chosen to be on the home page of Etsy, typically for around an hour each.

Vacation Mode: Sellers who need to put their shop on hold can choose to activate this mode, which hides all active listings from customers but lets the shop owner do any necessary behind-the-scenes work.

Index

About the Author

Gina Luker is the author of the popular DIY blog *The Shabby Creek Cottage* and owner of the successful Etsy shop The Shabby Creek Shop. She is a writer, photographer, and lover of all things handmade. Her work has been featured by Etsy and in many magazines, including *Brides Magazine, Somerset Home,* and *Romantic Homes.* She wades through life, one project at a time, alongside her husband and children.